LETTERS
TO
MARGARET

HUNTER DAVIES is a prolific author, journalist and broadcaster who has written for *Punch*, the *New Statesman*, *Guardian* and *Sunday Times*. He is the author of more than 100 books, including the only authorised biography of The Beatles and biographies of Wordsworth, Beatrix Potter and Alfred Wainwright. He spent every summer in the Lake District for nearly half a century and his *Lakeland: A Personal Journey* was published by Head of Zeus in 2016. He now divides his time between North London and the Isle of Wight.

ALSO BY HUNTER DAVIES
and published by Head of Zeus

Lakeland:
A Personal Journey

The Heath:
My Year on Hampstead Heath

Love in Old Age:
My Year in the Wight House

At the end of almost every day of their fifty-five years of married life, the author Margaret Forster would ask her husband, the naturally gregarious and outgoing Hunter Davies, to tell her about the events of his day: the gossip, the fun, the intrigues and the tribulations. In the years since Margaret's death in 2016, Hunter has continued to keep in touch, at least in his head. *Letters to Margaret* comprises a sequence of letters he wrote to her, mainly in 2022 and 2023. They contain accounts of his recent experiences and relationships, reflections on health and family matters, and also shared memories recalled by 'the one who should have died first'. Ultimately, they show how conversations with your loved one can, in a way, transcend death and continue to comfort the living.

CONTENTS

LETTER ONE

Barbados, 1986. Our first trip to the West Indies. Margaret and I flew there on Concorde to celebrate my fiftieth birthday.

Ashes to Ashes

Hiya, pet! Long time no see.

That is not just one of my typical bad-taste, thoughtless remarks, when I think I am being funny but it comes out as hurtful and silly. The sort you said I was always making. This one has an element of truth.

When you died, in February 2016, I did keep seeing you for a year. I would come home from my walk on the Heath, or swimming, or shopping, letting myself in the back way, through the garage, which you always said was stupid as it only saved a few yards compared with going out of the front door. And I was always seeing you.

I would walk across the lawn, then look through the dining-room window, and imagine you were there, lolling on your sofa, your feet up, reading a novel. You read a novel a day, always a new one, usually by a new young female novelist. I knew it would always be a novel.

I would open the back door and say 'Hi', still half believing you were in the house because I had seen you through the window.

After fifty-five years of marriage, so many of them spent in this house since 1963, it was not surprising that I imagined you were still here. Your presence was ever-present. Now, six years later, I don't have these imagined sightings as often as I did. But traces of you, evidence of your taste and decisions, are still all around.

I scattered half your ashes in Loweswater, where we had such a lovely rural life for thirty years. The other half is under the summerhouse at the bottom of this garden. You have probably forgotten that six weeks or so before you died, as you were on your last legs, unable to do any more of your enormous Heath walks, I suggested we have a summerhouse at the bottom of the garden. I wanted it in that dark corner, overshadowed by the ancient damson tree, where nothing ever seemed to grow. I said it would be a good place to have a summerhouse for you to use. It would give you an object, something to aim for as you staggered down the garden, somewhere to sit down in the shade. I thought it was such a Good Idea I contacted B&Q to see what they had. I was just thinking of an off-the-peg, simple, cheapo summerhouse, which I could probably erect myself.

'NO, NEVER!' you shouted. You were not having any work done in this house or in this garden, ever again. 'Over my dead body are we having a summerhouse.'

So I did what you requested. Unlike me, don't say it…

Six weeks later, you were dead. Six months later, I was walking down the garden and I thought, hmm, it would be a nice thing to have something in the garden to amuse the grandchildren. And when I get old and housebound, unable to walk on the Heath, or anywhere, I will be able to have a little toddle down the garden by myself and sit in my summerhouse.

So I bought one, off the peg. A nice Romanian lorry driver delivered it and kindly took it through the house and dumped it in the back yard. Took him ages as it was enormous. It was in a huge flat pack. I looked at it in horror. I am never going to assemble that, I told the man. Did he know anyone who erected summerhouses? He said he did, in his spare time, at the weekend, as a private job. He would put it up for me this Sunday, for £80. I agreed at once. He said his name was Arnold, which didn't sound very Romanian. And I have been there. Come on, pet, you have ten seconds to remember. Sorry, time's up. I went there in December 1971 for Spurs v Rapid Bucharest in the UEFA Cup when I was writing *The Glory Game*. Martin Chivers got three goals across the two legs. Now you remember.

When the summerhouse was erected, Flora put up sweet little curtains, and Richard connected electricity from the garage. I then had a street party, to officially unveil the summerhouse. All the local families with kids. The younger grandchildren, Amarisse and Sienna, and two of their little friends, did a dance to awful loud pop music and then acted out a play – which mainly consisted of them chasing each other round the corner – while all the adults sat drinking white wine. Chardonnay, I think. Quite smart at the time. Now I hate it. Everyone now drinks Sauvignon Blanc. Funny how times and tastes change. Remember when we got married and had friends in, we always gave them a glass of dry sherry. Sounds so quaint. Almost like something out of Jane Austen.

After the kids had entertained us, I made a speech. I always do these days, on any excuse. Just try to stop me. Not like when I was young. It comes with age and total confidence that I can ad lib and be awfully amusing. And if I am not, do I care? Do I heck.

In my speech, I revealed that half of your ashes are buried under the summerhouse. I then recalled what you had said – about how you were having a summerhouse over your dead body. Some of the older, stuffier neighbours made faces, but most people laughed. Yes, another bad-taste joke, I am afraid.

These days, walking up the garden and into the house, I don't see you as often as I did back in 2016. But walking the other way, out of the house and down the garden and into the mews, I pass the summerhouse and I always think, I hope Marg is keeping an eye on me.

Today, in fact, I have three summerhouses. Daft, I know. And, oh God, I have bought another house. I can't wait to tell you all the things I have done since you died – the places I have been, the ladies I have entertained in this very house, my various health dramas. I am sure you will be appalled by some of my behaviour.

But I hope you will enjoy it, my darling, when I tell you every little detail of what has happened to me since 2016. You always loved it when I came home and told you what had happened on the bus. 'Guess what, coming home on the C2 today – no, hold on, it is now the 88, or was it the 214...?' And you would shout at me: 'I don't care which bus it was! Just get on with the bloody story!'

You chose a pretty good time to scarper, back in 2016. You have missed very little since. You have avoided Brexit, Trump, Covid, Boris, Ukraine, Truss – don't ask who she was, everyone has already forgotten – economic crises, political corruption, police misconduct, inflation, shortage of avocados, the UK falling in all the world leagues – we are now down to nineteenth in the 2023 World Happiness Report, behind Iceland! Oh God, so many awful dreary things. You have been well out of it.

I find it hard to think of many cheerful or uplifting national happenings and world events since 2016. The England women's team winning the Euro football championship in 2022, that was good – and it certainly did cheer me up. You would have enjoyed the Queen's funeral later the same year. 'Enjoy' is perhaps not the word, but you know what I mean. You always found state occasions and royal pomp and circumstance entertaining. And you were an expert on the Royal Family, could spot and give the age of even the minor members, which always surprised some people, given your image of being a serious literary lady.

I hope by writing mainly about my life since you went, and about the family, and our friends, and the house, not forgetting the tortoise, I'll be able to entertain and inform and amuse you. There have been some changes, and some surprises and unexpected turns of events. Perhaps some of my recent behaviour might even appal you, but I will take that chance. You do know me...

So, here goes... Please do concentrate xxx

LETTER TWO

Margaret as a little girl in Carlisle, aged five.
Wistful, but doesn't she look bright?

Looking for a Chum

Hi again, Marg.

You did like gossip and chat, which used to surprise some people. But I knew how you loved *EastEnders* and *Casualty*, which I have never watched in my life – and loved me going out and coming home with all the goss. You liked hearing it, but you did not like foraging for it. I was always the social one, talking to everyone. You were more private. I often observed what you did if you were walking down our street and saw a neighbour coming the other way. You would pretend to have forgotten something, and turn back the other way, or cross over the street. There was always enough going on in your head, imagining other lives, to keep you amused, occupied and stimulated. Unlike me. I need the stimulus of other people.

It was quite a help to you, I suppose, in your last couple of housebound years. You never complained, never said you missed company. All you really wanted was your family – and another new novel to read. I am so different. I yell and wave at people in the street when they are miles away and have not seen me yet. 'How are you?' 'How are you doing?' 'What's happening?' 'I like your new hairdo.' If I see a hole in the ground, workmen digging, a crowd of people gathered, I rush to have a gawp and ask what's going on. Then come home and give you the gen.

I suppose that is the biggest thing I have missed these last six years – having you to talk to, to tell things to, then listen to your reactions and opinions. I could never quite predict how you would react, but in those fifty-five years – sixty, counting our courting years – we never actually stopped talking. Who says 'courting' these days? The word feels positively archaic. Most evenings when I am here in this house on my own, having my lonesome meal, I look down on myself from the ceiling and I think: 'How did this happen?' How come I am on my own in this house? No one to talk to, walk with, cuddle in bed, moan to. I am not lonely, but I am alone. And I still don't like it.

God knows, I have tried to get a companion, female of course, someone to share things with, possibly my life. And for a while, I got pretty near to achieving it. And perhaps I have now. To learn more about that, you'll have to read on.

I remember saying to you in the hospice, when I was moaning on about being on my own in the house for four weeks, which had seemed like a lifetime, how lonely I was… You looked at me, through me, really, as you always knew me so well. And you sighed. 'You will be fine. I have no worries about you at all, least of all about you being lonely.'

I have often thought of your words since. They cheer me up when nothing seems to have been happening, or I am bored, or my ideas and projects and approaches are being rejected. In your last six years, when you started all the awful treatment and drugs, after the cancer had got into your spine, you could not go on a plane anymore, but you encouraged me to go on my own to the West Indies each January, as we had always done since 1986.

We first went there on my fiftieth birthday: 7 January 1986. All my birthdays in my childhood and youth had been in the freezing cold of our Carlisle council house, which was so parky that if you put your bare feet on the linoleum floor, you could be stuck there till spring. As you will remember. I shared the bed with my younger brother Johnny, who did at least help to warm the bed a bit.

We went to the West Indies, to Cobblers Cove in Barbados, and then returned, year after year, for about a quarter of a century. 'You must go,' you said. 'I don't want to have your life ruined as well as mine. Please go. I don't care what you do there... as long as you come back.' So for six years I went to the Caribbean every January on my own. I had a good time as I knew so many of the regulars who always went for the same few weeks. They always invited me to their table for supper or to go on outings with them.

When you died, on 6 February 2016, I had not been that year, as I was visiting you every day in the hospice. I promised myself I might go later in the year. But I found I had so much to do – there was probate to organise, then getting all your manuscripts and diaries together to hand over to the British Library. Then I had the problem of Loweswater. What was I to do with the house where we had lived for several months every year for thirty years? We both loved it passionately. We felt at ease there, felt it was where we really belonged. You, at least, were a true-born Cumbrian. I was just pretending, having arrived there from Scotland when I was four.

I spent a summer there on my own. Which was a bit sad and pathetic, seeing you in every room. Every time I came in from a walk to the lake or shopping in Cockermouth, I would shout: 'Hi, Marg, I'm home.'

The house was stunning but pretty isolated, surrounded by fields and fells, plus three lakes within walking distance. I offered it to the children, but none of them wanted to take it on. They loved the Lake District, and had enjoyed many holidays there in their childhood, but they are Londoners born and bred, with their own houses and families and friends who live and work in London.

So, after my stay there on my own in the summer of 2016, as I had no partner or friend I wanted to take there, I sold it. I gave all the proceeds to the children – who went on to buy a seaside home in Broadstairs. You would love it. It is called Tait Cottage – named after Archibald Tait, who was Archbishop of Canterbury in the nineteenth century. It is in the grounds of what was once the Archbishop of Canterbury's summer palace.

Archibald Tait was Scottish born, like me, and was a former Dean of Carlisle. In fact, there is still a Dean Tait's Lane near Carlisle Cathedral and the library where we used to meet. We must have walked down Tait Lane hundreds of times. Once I discovered the Carlisle connection, I said to them: 'That's it, go for it.' And we have all loved it ever since.

Around nine months after you died, towards the year end, I was beginning to think I wanted to find some sort of chum. I didn't want to be on my own forever. I would like someone to do things with, go places with. In my fantasy, she would be sixty-five to seventy-five, single, widowed or divorced, with her own house, her own family, her own friends, having had her own career – and with her own teeth. This was really a euphemism. It meant she should be fit and well… and up for enjoying life to the full.

I wrote this, as a joke, in a column I was doing in *The Sunday Times* at the time, and it drew a few letters. One woman, who lived in Margate, said she owned a fish shop and could offer me fresh fish every day, if I was interested. I politely declined.

But there was a Brighton woman who had written to me earlier, out of the blue, to say we had met many years ago when she was in publishing. Would I like to meet for a drink some time? She had loved all your books and had just read your obituary. She sent her photo and looked quite attractive, but I could not actually remember her. I put her off, saying I was so busy at the moment, with probate and stuff, but might contact her in a few months. How kind.

You would not believe how much space your death got in the British – and American – press and I felt so proud. You would have just shrugged and dismissed it, said it must have been a quiet news day with nothing much else happening.

I was beginning to tell all my friends that I would now quite like a female chum, but I was also telling myself I did not want to get married again or even live with a woman. Just to have a regular companion. I considered myself to be married to you. And I still do. So why would I want to marry someone else? If I ever did, which I won't, I am sure you would probably not mind. You would consider it natural for a gregarious, social person like me. But in my head, you will always be my wife. I will really always be married to you.

By the way, my wedding ring has still not turned up. The one I lost in the garden twenty years ago when I was pruning the apple tree. You said at the time: 'Oh yeah, I bet you lost it deliberately.' I was rather hurt by that. Oh yes, I do have my feelings.

Eventually, after about three months, I wrote back to the woman who had sent me her photo and believed we had once met. I invited her for lunch when she next came to London. I took her to my local restaurant, Bistro Laz, beside the Heath, where I take all my visitors for lunch (it saves me the faff of going into town), but I did not tell her where I lived. She had written to me at *The Sunday Times* and they had forwarded it. I am still writing my so-called funny column in the Money pages every month, but I never go into the office.

We got on well and she invited me back to her house near

Brighton. Then she stayed with me. And that was it. We met every week from then on. Either she came here to my house or I went to hers. We had a lovely time together. For the next two years, I thought: 'That's it, sorted. I am settled with a companion for the rest of my life...'

Or was I? You are clever and probably already making shrewd guesses.

LETTER THREE

Margaret aged eleven, just about to pass the eleven-plus (a rare feat at her primary). She was the talk of the school – not because of her eleven-plus success, but because of her savagely cropped hair.

The End of the Affair

Wotcha, Marg.

I left you on a cliffhanger there... I think I suddenly had
something urgent to do. Oh, I know, football on the telly.
Spurs were playing live. Football is all I ever watch on the
telly. Just like the old days.

I was the only one who ever called you Marg. Everyone
always called you Margaret – at school, college and elsewhere.
Most Margarets tend to get called Maggie, such as Maggie
Thatcher and also Maggie Drabble, your exact contemporary
and fellow novelist.

I remember in about 1956 when you had scholarship
interviews at both Oxford and Cambridge, by chance you
happened to meet another girl called Margaret in both places.
In Oxford, you had some time to spare between interviews,
and the other Margaret offered to take you to a Quaker
meeting house. You didn't know what it was but found it
fascinating. When you came back to Carlisle, I wanted to
know how the interviews had gone, but you just wanted to
talk about the Quaker meeting, how struck you were by the
silence – no music, no talking.

The second Margaret was Maggie Drabble, though I never
took in her surname at the time. She was at a fee-paying
Quaker boarding school near York, and came from a middle-
class family, unlike you. But you were both offered open
scholarships to Oxford *and* Cambridge. You chose Oxford,

while Maggie chose Cambridge. So you never did become chums. But you met now and again at literary events, over the decades.

But back to my girlfriend. Any road up, as we say in football, it all seemed to be going well. We had two weeks in the West Indies in 2019. Remember how we both loved it there? It was club-class flights, five-star hotel, no expense spared. I know how to treat a gal.

But then it all went wrong... our relationship collapsed.

On our way home, at Gatwick railway station, we parted. I gave her a peck on the cheek and said thanks for the two years, as I really had enjoyed them. Have a good life. Bye bye. And that was it.

Yes, I know, I do these impulsive things. All my life. All *our* lives. Nothing has changed...

When I got home, I told Caitlin and Flora what had happened. They thought I was totally potty. I seemed to have been happy with her, and we got on, had good times together, went to lots of places.

I tend to reveal almost everything to almost everyone, whether they have asked for it or not, but it was a bit awkward to explain all the details to my own daughters. Jake, of course, being a man, had no interest in what happened either way. I explained to the girls that I may be old, but I do expect a proper relationship.

The next day, without consulting me, Caitlin organised a subscription to Saga Connections as a present for my forthcoming birthday on 7 January.

After you died, and I eventually thought I would like a female chum, I had dismissed the idea of online dating. At my age? And anyway, I did not want to meet strangers. I believed there must be enough women in my past who had got to my stage in life and were single and looking for what I am looking for. I am bound to come across a suitable one at some stage, someone I have met or vaguely met in the past.

Caitlin, as you know, found her partner online about seventeen years ago now, after she had returned from Botswana and her marriage had collapsed. We were both a bit surprised at the time. Not appalled, just surprised. The concept of online dating seemed alien to people of our generation. Caitlin and Nigel are still together and still happy after all these years. Though Caitlin has rather changed her life, which I will tell you about later, in another letter. I want to bash on with this online dating saga first. So don't interrupt.

I hate doing anything on the internet. I can never understand the instructions and the language – and my little fingers are now so stiff I keep pressing the wrong key. The other day I ordered 100 tins of tuna in olive oil from Tesco online instead of 10. Good job they will keep.

I filled in my Saga dating profile, told the truth about my age, eighty-four, and used a fairly recent photo – but of course not my real name or address. I called myself Eddie, for reasons you will understand.

What happens on Saga is– Are you listening? Please don't doze off – You have to answer a sequence of set questions about yourself, complete your profile, saying what sort of person you are looking for, then send it to some central point. Other people can access this and check you out, but they can't yet contact you directly.

The system analyses your details, likes and dislikes, and then analyses all of the women online and their details, likes and dislikes, and sends you something called 'matches'.

There were quite a few women I liked the look of from their photos and their basic biographical details, but the personal stuff was all so boring. They, too, had provided answers to the same questions and ticked the same set of multiple-choice answers, but the choices were so limited and banal. When asked about their financial circumstances, almost all ticked the same box: 'comfortable'. When asked what they were looking for, it was always 'companionship'. There was little hint of personality or real motivation and desires.

I had tried to make my profile as amusing as possible, and eventually a lot of replies came in. But I don't think that my profile content was the real reason for that. I was told by someone that women looking for blokes at my stage in life far outnumber men. Women live longer and they get widowed and divorced. There are therefore more women in the market than men. Lucky men.

Then I made personal contact with several women. This involves asking any interesting-looking matches if they will give you their phone number or email. And they do the same. Then you can have a chat, hear their real voice, decide if the person really exists and is not making it all up. If that goes well, over a few weeks, you might arrange to meet, or have coffee perhaps.

In the space of one week, I arranged to see five ladies at the bistro – not at the same time, of course, on different days. After their Christmas hols and New Year gatherings, I think all the single people out there were suddenly keen to get on with real life.

Two of them, when they sat down, said the same thing: 'I have a confession to make…' Goodness, I thought, what can this be? Are they married? Or have changed gender? 'I am not sixty-five. I'm seventy-three.' I laughed aloud. Such vanity.

One of them was a GP in Highgate, which I thought beforehand would be brilliant: a new lady friend living locally and on tap to minister to all my needs. What could be neater? Over the meal we chatted away, and I heard her life story, which was interesting. But after ten minutes' conversation, I decided she was away with the fairies, if not totally potty. So I paid the bill, and that was that. I never heard from her again. She obviously could not see any future with me either. Probably thought I was potty as well.

Another was a retired deputy headmistress of a private school, who had been at Oxford, at your old college, in fact. You know I always liked clever women, but she was a parody of a teacher, with a booming voice, and much too hearty and jolly hockey sticks.

I quite liked three of the five I invited for lunch and they each invited me back to their house for a meal. One turned out to have had a career in the media, but on the advertising side. I liked her, she was interesting and attractive, and I liked her house. Alas, when I happened to mention I was looking for someone to go on holiday with, she said lovely, but she made it clear it would have to be separate bedrooms. Oh dear.

I saw one of these three several times over a period of a few weeks. We ate together at restaurants near her house, and I stayed the night. We had good fun, a pleasant time – but there was not really a connection. I could see no future in it.

And then my old girlfriend suddenly reappeared. She said that in the West Indies she had been ill, felt rotten. When she came back to London, she had to have a minor operation. She was sorry.

I had missed her, so we agreed to meet on neutral ground, on a park bench, to discuss things. She said she would like to get back together, as long as I gave up the online dating. Some kind girlfriend of hers had spotted me on Saga dating. I said yes, of course I would put a stop to it.

And so we resumed our relationship. And I thought it was lovely. We were back to how we were. I still felt I was married to you, and would be forever, but then I got really carried away. I gave her a large sum of money to pay for some work on her house that she was desperate to do. I still can't believe I did it.

Then I did something mad. Foolish old men, eh? Swayed by the love of an attractive younger woman, which she was, and rather glamorous.

We had had some great times at the cottage in Broadstairs, but whenever the weather was really good, we were in competition with the three children and their families to stay there. It was their cottage anyway, not mine; it was in their names and they paid all the bills.

We decided it would be wonderful to have our own cottage, just for us, in a new place that neither of us knew. The location we decided upon was the Isle of Wight. Maybe we were subliminally influenced by the Beatles lyric in 'When I'm Sixty-Four'? We would find something not too dear, live properly together there for the first time, all lovey-dovey. We would keep our respective homes but from now on would spend half of our lives on the Isle of Wight. Like you and I did for those thirty years in the Lake District.

So, in the early autumn of 2020, bang in the middle of the coronavirus pandemic (I'll try to explain this later, promise), we found a cottage on the Isle of Wight, just a few minutes from a marvellous sandy beach, on the flat, unlike Broadstairs. I paid for it, put it in my name, but she did all the renovating, furnishing, décor, painting. And she made it look wonderful. I loved it there – the cottage, the island, the people, our new friends – and I always will. But then the same thing happened again. It started to go wrong.

We staggered on for a few weeks. Then she went home earlier than we had planned, on her own, in her car, leaving me to return on my own on the train, which I hate doing. She said that since we were arguing all the time, and making each other unhappy, she might as well go home. Oh God.

You and I, when we were young, had lots of arguments, but of a different sort. When we were first courting, and still students, you used to say, 'I am never getting married.' I would reply, 'Who is asking you, pet?' Then you would say you were never going to have any children, the world is too horrible a place to bring more children into it. Again, I said, 'Who is asking you?' Worst of all, you used to say it would never work. That you were bad for me, you were a horrible person, you would make me unhappy. I would tell you not to be stupid, of course you don't make me unhappy.

But it did worry and depress me. I thought, because you were so clever and intuitive, that perhaps you were right. You were also so good on people's motives and feelings. When you went on about our relationship being pointless, how it would never work, I tried to ignore you, or I told myself you were just testing me.

At the time, we seemed to be constantly arguing, but looking back it was probably over a period of just a few months. Then, for no reason I can remember, it settled down; you never said those things again. We did not talk about it openly, or even discuss our future. It just seemed to happen, that we both accepted this was it, we were going to be together forever, this was love. Not that we ever used such soppy words.

Of course, I got very worried when you went to Oxford. I thought some tall, handsome, blond, floppy-haired public schoolboy would sweep you off your feet. You starred in an Oxford play with Dennis Potter, which I came from Durham to see, and I read the rave reviews. Even today, whenever I meet Richard Ingrams, he tells me how he fell in love with you as Grusha in *The Caucasian Chalk Circle*.

Fortunately for me, you did not get swept off your feet by some Adonis. In fact, the opposite happened. You always said you disliked Oxford and particularly the men: they were so childish and immature, knew nothing about real life. You could not wait to leave Oxford, which was why we got married the day after your last exams. You were technically still a student and the principal, Dame Janet Vaughan, had to give you special permission.

Anyway, I split up with my girlfriend. The fun and affection seemed to have gone out of the relationship and we were always arguing.

This all happened over a year ago now. What have I been doing since, you ask? Good question.

I will keep you up to date with developments and report progress... if there is any.

LETTER FOUR

Margaret aged fifteen by the River Eden,
near Carlisle, posing for her brother Gordon,
an apprentice photographer.

Meeting People

Hello again, my one and only love heart. Sorry for the silence these last few weeks. Not much to report really.

This time I had no intention of doing online dating, though two years earlier it had led to some enjoyable encounters. I felt I was too old and too tired for all that. I should hang up my boots, settle myself, give up all hopes of a proper relationship ever again, not at my age. I should just grow up, be content and lead a celibate existence from now on.

I do, after all, have loads of lady friends, chums from the neighbourhood or people I have worked with in publishing and newspapers who have always kept in touch with me and with whom I have regular lunches. I love them all, we have some laffs, but of course no hanky-panky. All platonic. Most of them are happily married.

So I told myself I am going to be quiet and sensible, act my age, not like a crazed teenager anymore. Love in old age, if you are fortunate enough to have it, is really like love in any age, teenage or otherwise. You still get carried away, on a high, then get downhearted when she has not called or emailed you. You try to work out what it means. What are her real motives? Does she really love me? What have I done to upset her? And then you act irrationally, do daft things you regret. Oh God, do I need any of that ever again? I have had a good run, a good life, sixty marvellous years with you. Why be greedy?

Do you believe any of this? Or do you think I am talking bollocks? That I really will never settle down and be sensible. As long as I have the breath to cool my porridge, as my mother used to say.

Yes. I think you could be right. You know me too well. I have never taken no for an answer. So I have now made a vow to myself to say yes to everything, yes to life, and to accept any suggestion of drinks or meals, as long as it does not mean having to travel anywhere, such as into town.

In London, I have just this week cancelled my membership at the Groucho Club. I am sure you will be pleased, as you never liked it. We were founder members and shareholders when it all began in 1985. Our silver wedding anniversary celebration at the Groucho was their first-ever private party. Melvyn Bragg made a nice speech and I invited Shiva Naipaul – V. S. Naipaul's younger brother – which you thought was awful, as I had only just met him. But he did come and he enjoyed himself. He died just a month or so later, aged only forty. What a tragedy.

Since you died, I have had other parties at the Groucho – for my eightieth birthday, for my hundredth book. But I have not been there for over three years – and not just because of Covid. It's because I have got lazy and traffic has got worse and I hate trailing into town. Instead, I persuade people to come here, to see my house and my treasures. I give them a drink, and then we walk out the back into the mews and on to the Heath and have lunch at the bistro, which I pay for, as I have dragged them all the way out here...

I have been managing to invite somebody here for lunch once a week. Preferably of the female persuasion, but not always. I am not sexist. Shall I tell you who my guests and lunch companions have been over the last few weeks? No need to think about it, pet. You know I'm going to tell you anyway.

JAMIE

This week, let me think, I invited Jamie from the British Library. I've known him for years. He was head of manuscripts when I first handed over my Beatles manuscripts to them. He introduced me at various BL talks events over the years. I get on well with him. His wife is an academic, but I've not met her. He has since been promoted to some corporate-sounding position, still at the BL, and is now in charge of several departments.

Over lunch, he told me how he is involved in setting up a brand-new branch of the BL in the north. They have acquired a magnificent nineteenth-century factory building in Leeds, which looks stunning – he brought the glossy brochure to show me. All they need is £25m. He will run it, when it eventually opens. He asked if I thought Macca would give some money as it is a northern project. I said to Jamie I wasn't sure, as he has no connection with Leeds.

SARAH

Then I had lunch with Sarah. You will remember her and her husband, Kevin; they were always at Cobblers Cove in Barbados when we were. When you died, they kindly invited me to their home in Mallorca. It was nice to catch up on their life and their daughter's, whom I also met. I hope to keep in contact...

MATT

Matt is features editor of the *Daily Express*. He had been suggesting lunch for ages, hoping I would write something for them. But I am such a snob. I only like writing for papers that I read. Nothing against the *Express*. My parents loved the *Express*, they read it every day. My theory is that all owners and most editors are bastards – but you don't write for them, you write for the line manager, the person you know and like. Matt came to my Heath book launch (my love letter to Hampstead Heath and to you) and I wrote a piece for him about the book. For our lunch at the bistro, he arrived on a skateboard. First newspaper executive I have known to do that. Or any adult really…

BECKY

News editor of *The Sunday Times*, whom I adore. She was my boss on the Money pages for several years. I told her not to take the news editor job. The reporters will hate you, you will have to shout at them – and in my long career I have never known of a news editor ever becoming editor. But she is loving it. She cancelled coming here, as she was so busy, so I went to see her at London Bridge, the massive modern block that is HQ of the *ST* and *The Times*. She took me to lunch in Borough Market – which was amazing; I'd not been there for about fifty years. Then we came back to the *Sunday Times* office and went round the news floor. Vast. All these poor sods stuck side by side at their screens, like battery hens. Not like in my day, when we had oak-panelled offices and personal secretaries. I met the new *ST* editor, Emma, and the *Times* editor, John Witherow, though I knew him already. He was the one who got me to do my Money column, twenty-odd years ago. Becky is married to a maths teacher who is an amazingly supportive husband. Three kids, quite young, all at state schools – hurrah. God knows how she manages her job, but she has Tuesday and Wednesday at home. She was so cheerful and nice. A grand lunch. Loads of media gossip.

JACKIE

Jackie came for coffee. She and her husband, Stephen, were friends and neighbours in the next street for fifty years. You liked them. They came to all our parties when our kids were small. *Now* you remember him. Anyway, I happened to be on the bus with him last year, going to Kentish Town, and by chance sat down beside him. He said how excited he was because the next day he and Jackie were off to India. Lucky beggar, I said. But during the flight, he had a stroke. The plane had to make an emergency landing. This was over a year ago. I have visited him a couple of times, in a hospital at St Pancras and then a nursing home in the Muswell Hill area.

He is now back home but has still not recovered. He's in a wheelchair, housebound, needs round-the-clock help, can't talk, but seems to understand what Jackie says. Amazingly, he has a singing teacher who comes to the house and sings *Lieder* with him – in German. Stephen can still remember the words. Isn't that wonderful? When Dorothy Wordsworth was gaga, and had what was probably dementia, she would sit by the fireside in Dove Cottage and recite dear William's poetry for hours. When my mother had Alzheimer's, she would get us all to sing Scottish songs with her. You never know what is round the corner. Live while you can.

JOANNA

Joanna Trollope is my fellow judge of the Isle of Wight Book Awards, along with Alan Titchmarsh. She came here to London to talk about the awards. I did like her. We got on so well. She has been married twice, is now single, with two daughters, whom she visits a lot. She lives in rented accommodation in south London. Strange, when she must be so well off, but she now hates the flat, thinks it was a mistake to have rented it. She has invited me back for lunch in February. We had so much in common, and got on so well. She reminded me a lot of you – and not just because of Oxford and writing novels. There did seem to be a spark between us, but she made it clear she was not interested in relationships anymore. She has done all that. Ah well. We shall see.

LADY KATE

Another one I really like. She's the widow of a Labour life peer I knew. They had a house locally and one in Barbados, next to Cobblers Cove. I met her with him once, many years ago, when he was still alive. Then out of the blue I got a fan letter from her about my Heath book – so I invited her over. Lovely woman. We have so many friends in common as she was a publisher for many years. She lives in Hampstead, in the best part. Alas, she has a partner, a Conservative peer, to whom she might get married. Ah well. So we will just be good friends, eh.

PROFESSOR ANN

Lives locally, well-known author, feminist and academic, known her to say hello to for decades, once met her at a book thing, but never had a proper chat with her. She came to my garden party for sixty people to celebrate our sixty years in this house. Did I tell you about it? Oh, it was fab. Richard did the barbecue, with Jake's help. I had live music, played by the jazz guitarist John Etheridge – very upmarket. Ann was at the party and had a few drinks and became quite vivacious. I later invited her for lunch and we got on well. She has parted from her husband. I hope to see her again. Who knows...

DAVID

David is from the Vale of Health – he lives in the house where you and I rented a flat after we got married in 1960. While I was writing my book about Hampstead Heath, in 2020, I wrote to David explaining our past association with the house and we made a date for me to have tea there. My visit ended up generating a whole chapter in the book, and he and his wife later came to the launch of *The Heath* at Keats House. David also let me see something that you would have loved – a long letter from Mr Elton, our old landlord in the Vale of Health, whom we nicknamed 'Sedgers'. David had found it among the house documents when he got his hands on the deeds, and it was all about the house's recent rather tangled history.

Apparently, Mr Elton had inherited the house from a total stranger, and in turn would bequeath the house to someone he was not related to, a woman who happened to be renting the same flat we'd lived in. When he died, she discovered to her amazement that he had left the house to her. What Sedgers did not know was that the woman was having an affair with another lodger. After Sedgers' death, the pair got married, but within a short space of time they both died also. When David bought the house, he would experience endless complications because so many parties were involved. I wonder if you could have made a novel out of the story? Do you remember your novel *Mr Bone's Retreat*? Well, I can't, but I have a memory that you based the character on Sedgers.

PETE

Husband of my friend Caitlin Moran. He is a big Beatles fan, as is Caitlin. We had been in contact over the forthcoming *Get Back* film. He has been here before with Caitlin and one of their daughters. But he did the tour again, followed by the bistro lunch. We caught up on our respective families and on their two daughters – about whom Caitlin rarely writes in her *Times* magazine column. I do love the *Times* Saturday magazine. It's the best of all the colour mags. Pete used to be chief music critic for *The Times*. I loved chatting with him about his family, his wife, money and the media – four of my very favourite topics.

EM AND CATH

I think I have their names right… both were fellow guests at a Heath and Ham Society party. I happened to sit beside them. I thought at first they were mother and daughter – but they were old work colleagues who worked in the same publishing house.

Again, I found I had lots in common with them, because of publishing and media work. I invited the younger one back here to have lunch, see my garden and tortoise in the daylight and go to the bistro… yes, same old chat-up line. Mad really, as she could only have been about fifty. It turned out, of course, that she had a boyfriend. Ah well, I can but try.

When I have the energy I might tell you about my Isle of Wight encounters, of which there have been just as many. Yes, I have kept on the Isle of Wight house, for the moment anyway, as I still love going there, even on my own. And I do have lady friends down there, who are just as interesting, but unlike the London ones, you won't know any of them.

You are probably appalled at my inviting all these women to lunch, in London and the Isle of Wight. But you know me. When you live alone and have a singleton life, you are keen on almost any social intercourse. At least, I am. Unlike you, I have no shame and am not easily embarrassed by rejection...

LETTER FIVE

Margaret in her first year at Oxford, 1957, explaining something to somebody. Note the glass of beer. Not like her. Students, eh?

Walks Down Memory Lane

Hiya.

I walked for almost three hours this morning. Amazing. Most I have done for a long time. OK, there were lots of stops, and sit-downs, and coffees and visiting bookshops, but come on, three hours, respect, at my age. I also take lots of walks on the Isle of Wight – all of them seaside walks, along miles of sandy beaches, in and out of little coves – and all on the flat. With enough cafés and pubs to break up the walks with refreshments.

I wonder how long I will be able to keep this up. My knees are good at the moment but my back often gives me gyp. When I bend down I often can't get up, and when I do, I usually feel dizzy and have to sit down again. But I am not going to bang on about my health. You have been through all that enough already. I just count my blessings. The best of all by far was marrying you.

Firstly, I got the bus to Great Portland Street just after nine and walked across Harley Street and all those other medical streets, catering to the world's rich but ill. Streets that were mainly empty and lovely at that time of morning. I was able to stand in the road and look at the architecture.

I passed Wimpole Street, where Elizabeth Barrett used to live. I remember when you were working on her biography and we tried to find the house where the Barretts of Wimpole Street lived. But we failed to do so. I think it was bombed in the war.

41

Didn't we have some good trips together when you were doing non-fiction books? For your life of Elizabeth Barrett Browning, we went to Florence and visited Casa Guidi, where Elizabeth and Robert Browning lived. For your Bonnie Prince Charlie biog, we went to Rome.

And for my books, we had some even longer trips. Do you remember when I was doing my Robert Louis Stevenson book, we went to Samoa and to the Napa Valley in California? Wasn't that fun and exotic?

Today, I would not take on a book that involved any travelling – well, not outside London. I now hate going anywhere alone, especially having to stay in a strange place in a strange hotel on my own.

The other day, I went to Daunt Books in Marylebone High Street – capital of the Daunt empire. Amazing building. Not at all like W. H. Smith in Carlisle. It is an architectural gem, with galleries, balconies, skylights and stained-glass windows. I have been to lots of book launches there over the years for various friends and it is a fabulous location for a literary event.

It is a superior place – and the staff also tend to be a bit superior. To them, an author coming in is nothing. They made me feel that, by allowing me to sign copies of my Heath book, they were doing me a favour. I was then asked if I minded doing a little podcast, just chatting to the camera for five minutes. Apparently, they have lots of subscribers around the world who will watch such things and then perhaps be tempted to buy the book.

I asked them if I could tell a funny story, and they wanted to know which one. I said it's on page 156 of my Heath book, the chapter about visiting Keats House. 'As I was leaving, I saw a visitors' book and decided to read the last ten entries. Nine were from obviously well-brought-up young ladies from Singapore and Hong Kong, who have been to good

English-language schools and studied Keats. They all wrote much the same stuff... how they fell in love with Keats, his life was so romantic, it was a pilgrimage to come here, blah blah blah.

'The last entry was clearly from a teenage boy: "I love the fact that Keats had lots of Fannies in his life..." Adolescent humour, but a good Keats joke. His sister and mother were both called Fanny and he fell in love with a Fanny.' The assistant smiled at the story, but said: 'Please, *please*, do not use it. We have lots of Americans who follow us and they don't like anything rude...'

After Daunt's, I headed into Regent's Park, deciding I would walk all the way to my next appointment – at the Primrose Hill bookshop. I had forgotten how beautiful the Broad Walk is, so many flowers, shrubs and trees. It brought back so many memories. When I was presenting *Bookshelf* on BBC Radio 4 back in the 1980s (or was it the 1990s? Life has got concertinaed since you went), I used to walk back from Broadcasting House in Portland Place after I had recorded the programme. I often walked all the way home, through Regent's Park, Primrose Hill and then across the Heath. I could do it in fifty-five minutes. Couldn't do it in that time now.

On the way to Primrose Hill, I had several stops for a rest and a coffee and listened to all the French accents. So many French people seem to live around here these days. And near us in NW5 as well. Brexit does not seem to have put them off. And no wonder. The nice parts of London are so very nice – interesting, safe and pretty.

I am so lucky, still being here, alive to all that London has to offer. I loved Lakeland, and now the Isle of Wight, but when I am in either place, I often forget all the glories of London life.

Almost everywhere I go in central London I have memories of walking with you, exploring London, which was unknown to both of us when we got married in 1960 and had our first home in the Vale of Health. Today, over sixty years later, whenever I walk around London, I remember all the people I have interviewed or visited here.

Do you remember a supper we had in Regent's Park with Terence Conran and his then-wife Caroline? She was with me at *The Sunday Times*, doing the cookery stuff, when I was women's editor. She used to send her copy, beautifully typed out by her secretary, in a chauffeur-driven car.

I also had Jilly Cooper, Molly Parkin, Lucia van der Post and Lesley Garner on my staff. Such interesting women, such great long boozy lunches, such larks. I bought a fridge, at my own expense, so we could have cold drinks in the office, in what I called the Look suite. I got teased by my male friends on the paper about having so many lovely women on my staff; there were lots of nudge-nudge jokes. People thought I was having an affair with Molly. No chance. She would have eaten me alive. But I did really like Caroline Conran – though there was no affair.

That evening with her and Terence was strange. He said very little. I think they had had words. But I remember their house being stunning, a Georgian gem, overlooking the park.

Passing the Zoo, I could see the structure of the Snowdon bird cage. Later, when I edited the colour mag, Tony (known as Antony Armstrong-Jones until his marriage to Princess Margaret, after which he became Lord Snowdon) was one of the photographers. I did one job with him, interviewing and photographing the footballer Rodney Marsh. I had to pick Tony up at Kensington Palace, where he was living with Princess Margaret. He faffed about endlessly, changing his clothes, asking which would be the best outfit for snapping a famous footballer. He had never met one before. We finally decided on his safari suit.

We had to go to the Queens Park Rangers training ground, somewhere out west, where the team was training. I had agreed with Rodney that he would have his shower in a certain shower and Tony would take his picture.

While they were still on the pitch, Tony set up his gear in the shower and had me standing in it as he got his focus and lights correct and did some test shots. When the whistle blew, and training was over, Rodney came off and went straight to the shower, stripped off and turned on the water. Oh God. What a panic Tony was in. He had done his test shots with the water turned off. The minute the hot taps were turned on, the shower walls steamed up. He could see bugger all. Meanwhile, Rodney had finished showering and went into the dressing room to change. I had to go after him and persuade him to come back, explaining that there had been a technical fault. This time, Tony did the shower shots with no water on.

In Chalcot Square I admired the stunning house where Joan Bakewell used to live, and where we had supper with her and her husband of the time, a young bloke, a theatre director who fancied himself.

Do you recall the time we once looked at a flat in Chalcot Road? The children were about to be off our hands, going away to college. I got it into my head that we could live nearer central London and not have a car. I bullied you into looking at this flat, as you were never really keen on moving. We looked around it – lovely situation, quite spacious – but then I realised that in a flat you have people above and below and sideways, any of whom could turn out really noisy and annoying. Why did I not realise that beforehand? Whereas here in NW5 we are in a semi-detached house with a side passage and a garden front and back. I dropped the idea, much to your relief.

People always thought you were the strong, dominant one in

our marriage, because you were clearly so clever and direct. But you always maintained that I had made all the major decisions in our life. You were dead against me buying another house in our street. When my mother got dementia and couldn't live alone in Carlisle anymore, there was a vacant ground-floor flat in the house at number 29 that I thought would suit her. She would not live with us but just be 100 yards away. You said it was a stupid idea. There were two lots of sitting tenants above her who would drive me mad. Which was true. I regretted it. But they eventually left and, when my mother died, I sold the house at a good profit.

All the country cottages we bought, and our Portuguese house, were my doing – though you did enjoy them in the end. Come on, admit it. I planned all the holidays in the West Indies, pushing and bossing you around, when you said, really, you would rather stay at home. You really just wanted a quiet life. Whereas I am always on the go, with some plan, plot or project bubbling away in my mind.

After you died, I read all your diaries, which you wrote every fifth year, back to your schooldays, in your immaculate handwriting. I never read them at the time. They were not secret – the family knew you were writing them – but they were private and personal, placed securely in your bottom drawer. I never opened them, honestly.

I don't spy.

Not like you.

Oh yes you did.

You once told me you had read some notes on Caitlin's desk when she was still at school – a description of some awful visitor who had come to stay. It was the first sign that Caitlin might become a writer.

I went through all your diaries after you died, about a million words. Took me six months. They were going to the British Library and I wanted to make notes, explain the references, to help their cataloguers. There was one remark made in passing in 1980 that rather upset me: 'When exactly did Hunter become a hustler?' you asked yourself.

It was the word 'hustler' that upset me – making me sound dodgy and nasty and wicked. If you had said when did I become pushy and bossy, I would not have minded that. Others, including our children, have said much the same. Today, several of my lady friends have said it. I deny it, of course. In my mind, I am always affable, charming, have no strong opinions, easily give in, don't dislike anyone, am kind to animals and help old ladies across the road.

But I have to admit that my character underwent a sort of transformation from about the age of thirty. When I was young, when we first met, I was shy, tongue-tied, had no confidence. But everybody always says that about themselves. Then later I had a chip on my shoulder when I came to London and first worked on *The Sunday Times*, feeling inferior, a council-house provincial, among the clever Oxbridge graduates, most of whom seemed to have been president of the Oxford or Cambridge Union. I can't remember when those feelings faded. But they have. I think the change began to happen when I married you. Sorry about the arse-licking. Not much use now.

Back to my walk. I eventually reached Primrose Hill and the so-called village. Its pretty row of shops seems to consist mainly of coffee bars – there must be about twenty of them, their customers spilling out onto the pavement, even in mid-December. Most of them look and sound like tourists who have come to Primrose Hill in the hope of doing a bit of celebrity-spotting. The bookshop was very welcoming, compared with Daunt's, yet I had never signed books there before. The couple who own it seem nice – they live off Holloway Road, can't afford Primrose Hill. They offered me coffee, which has not happened at a bookshop signing before. And they let me use their lav.

The woman, Jessica, said she was pleased to meet me, as the father of Caitlin. She is a swimmer and has read Caitlin's books. She went to an event where Caitlin spoke and thought she was lovely. For so many decades I used to go to book events where people would say: 'Oh, is your wife with you? It's your wife I want to meet!' So now, for the rest of my life, will I be Caitlin's dad?

I seem to be rambling a bit. I don't expect you to read all of my letters. You must be sooo busy up there. Reading novels all day long, with no interruptions like having to make meals for your husband. You always used to say, when I was chuntering on: 'Do me a favour and don't talk for the next half hour.' I am writing these letters because I miss you so much, but also because I love sharing.

And I am now a single human being again, alas, with no one to share the trivia and humdrum of my day and all the flotsam floating around in my mind.

As a little boy growing up in Johnstone, I was just the same. Aged four, I would stand at the garden gate and stop passers-by, telling them who I was, what I was doing, and what my mother and father were arguing about. I have always liked to share things, whether people had asked me to do so or not. So I wanted to unload what I did today, just another walk, just another day. Tomorrow I won't remember any of it, what I did or what I thought.

I know that really, of course, these letters are for me. To try to make sense of my life now I am on my own. To communicate with myself. And with you. You always did listen…

See you later, alligator…

LETTER SIX

*On Hampstead Heath, 1960. We had just been
to see the flat in the Vale of Health we hoped to
move into after we got married.*

Get Back

Hey there, Georgy Girl...

You always hated any reference to that book, or the film, or the song, but I must tell you about attending a world première in Leicester Square.

It was a documentary about the Beatles: *The Beatles: Get Back*. The whole film was apparently going to be eight hours long on some pay-per-view service, but the première was a specially edited version, introduced by the director, Peter Jackson, before an invited audience.

I would have asked a girlfriend to come with me, if I still had one. They are generally up for any of the fancy occasions to which I have been invited in the last year or so, such as a box at the Albert Hall for a concert by the Royal Liverpool Philharmonic Orchestra, VIP tickets to the Chelsea Flower Show, a reception at 11 Downing Street, a private party at the Westminster home of Jacob Rees-Mogg. His mother, Gillian, as you probably remember, is an old friend of mine.

In fact, I am having lunch with Gillian next week. She is taking me to The Ivy. Gillian and I worked together at *The Sunday Times* back in the sixties. She was in the next-door office as secretary to William Rees-Mogg, the City editor. I was the assistant on the Atticus column, then run by Robert Robinson. Gillian was friendly with our secretary and, when Bob was out, they would sit in our office gossiping. Listening to them, while trying to work, I realised that Gillian was in love with William Rees-Mogg. One day, I overheard her saying she was going to resign, as William ignored her. Next day, when I met William in the corridor, I said: 'I gather Gillian is leaving.' 'Gillian who?' he asked. 'Your blooming secretary,' I replied. A month later, he proposed. I might have exaggerated the brevity of the time scale, but Gillian, when I remind her of the story, always smiles and says it is roughly true.

I wondered a long time about who to take with me to the *Get Back* film première, which was being held in Leicester Square in November 2021.

A week or so before the event, I got another invite, this time for a VIP post-première film party at a posh Soho restaurant. That sounded even more exclusive. But I still did not know whom to ask. I wondered about asking one of our two granddaughters, the big ones, Ruby and Amelia, both now twenty-two – yeah, amazing, I know! How did they get there?! They were just sixteen when you last saw them. I'll tell you about them later.

It got to the day before the première and I was beginning to think this is an awful faff, going into the West End in the evening on my own. Can I really be bothered? Then I thought of Denise.

I don't think I have told you I have a lodger. After you died, and I was living in this big house on my own, I felt embarrassed having all this space to myself. I did think of converting the top floor, where the children's bedrooms used to be, into a separate flat with its own entrance, with a staircase at the side. My plan was to offer it for free to a nurse at the Marie Curie hospice where you spent your last six weeks. I even mentioned it to your palliative care consultant, Philip, who had become a friend of mine. But Camden Council turned it down. Said it would count as another residence and I would need planning permission. Also, I would have to provide separate bike stands. Potty. So I did nothing. Left it empty for about a year. Instead, I gave a donation of £50k to Marie Curie, in your memory.

Then a friend from the past, whom we both knew, David Foster from Carlisle, who took over our Vale of Health flat after we moved to Dartmouth Park in 1962, said his daughter Kirsty, who is a doctor, was coming to London on secondment for six months. She needed a room for three nights a week. Did I have any space? I said of course. She turned out to be a consultant – very handy, I thought, when I get poorly, but her speciality was public health. Not much good to me. Not at the time. A year later, when the Covid virus came – sorry, pet, I know I promised to explain it, but it would just take too long – it would have been handy having a public health expert on the premises.

After Kirsty moved back to the north-east, I got another lodger, again recommended by David. Alison, who was married with two boys, was doing six months in London as a secretary at SOAS, University of London. I never had much chat with Kirsty the doctor. She just came home each evening and went straight upstairs. But if I was reading the evening paper and having a drink when Alison came home, I would say 'hi' and offer her a drink. We would then have a chat about her day. We got on so well that when I heard her husband and two sons were visiting London, I said they could stay here, in the flat. In her sitting room, which used to be Caitlin's bedroom, there is still the sofa that opens up into a double bed.

Then I had a much younger lodger: Paula, a Romanian, nanny to the actor Benedict Cumberbatch and his wife, who live in the next street.

After her came Denise. These four lodgers, all by chance women, just happened. I did not advertise. But Denise I did already know. You have met her as well. She is the sister of Caitlin's partner, Nigel. Denise works locally in a school in Hackney. Unlike the other three, she is generally at home here seven nights a week, unless it's the school hols. The other three only stayed part of the week. The nanny was away for three months when Benedict was filming in New Zealand. Denise has turned out to be a brilliant lodger. She keeps an eye on the house when I am away on the Isle of Wight. I never hear her coming in and out. And she is a dab hand with techie things when I have got in a state over my computer or mobile phone.

She had earlier told me that some years ago she had gone to the Isle of Wight Festival to see Paul McCartney – whom she loves. So I asked her if she would like to come with me to the première and afterwards to the VIP reception at Kettner's. She jumped at the chance.

We got lost in Leicester Square. God, what a nightmare that part of London is today, as crowded as Wembley Stadium on Cup Final day. Thousands of overexcited, well-off-looking kids, mostly from abroad.

Back in 1968, I had my own world film première in Leicester Square, *Here We Go Round the Mulberry Bush*, based on my novel of the same name. At the Odeon. I can't remember where you had your première for *Georgy Girl*. Leicester Square, probably. Anyway, you agreed to come with me to *Here We Go Round the Mulberry Bush*. Very kind of you. But you made no comments about it. Yes, rubbish screenplay (written by me) but a fun film with great music. It was a red-carpet affair, and all the Beatles turned up in their fab gear.

As Denise and I wandered round and round Leicester Square, Denise eventually got out her mobile and tracked down the location of Cineworld, which I had never heard of. We got in, with our tickets, and were immediately given glasses of champagne, which we were allowed to take to our seats. So civilised. Then we settled down to watch *Get Back*.

It was introduced on screen by Peter Jackson. I started groaning under my breath, 'Get on with it, stop showing off, come on, you have just repackaged loads of old tape, which all of us Beatles fans have known about for decades. The person who should be getting all the credit is Michael Lindsay-Hogg, who shot the original footage, especially the brilliant Savile Row rooftop session.'

Paul McCartney himself turned up, suddenly appearing on stage in front of the screen at the end of the showing, with his daughter Mary.

Afterwards, Denise and I and a hundred or so other VIP guests walked round the corner and made for Kettner's. Paul arrived, looking fit and well and thin and was ever so charming and friendly with all the other guests. He has always been good at glad-handing, nice and polite to all the fans and old friends. John would soon have been telling them to fuck off.

I introduced Paul to Denise, saying, 'This is my lodger.' 'Oh yeah, Hunt,' he said, giving me a nudge and a poke in the ribs.

Paul and I talked about the film and I said I had spotted Michael, his brother, in one shot. He said he loved the film – it brought back all the laughs, before it all ended in tears.

I also talked to Pattie Boyd, first wife of George Harrison. Do you remember she and George came to our house for tea – or was it supper? – when I was doing the Beatles biog? She was looking gorgeous. She was carrying slightly more weight than in the sixties, but aren't we all? Apart from Paul. He looked the same weight as ever. I asked Pattie why she was not in the film – I mean, not in the shots on the roof at Savile Row. 'George wouldn't let me go. He said it would be boring for me.' She said she was working on a book of her photographs

– and asked if I would help her. I said: 'Yes, come for tea, pet. I am still in the same house which you and George visited, fifty-five years ago.'

I also talked to Terry Gilliam and Mick Hucknall, no longer a flaming redhead, but he has still got hair. He was with his daughter. I last met him at Downing Street at a Tony Blair reception. Mick and I happened to go up the stairs together and talked about the Beatles for most of the evening.

Everyone was of course jostling to buttonhole Paul. I found a comfy sofa and sent Denise off for drinks and food. She came back to say she had spotted Brian Cox, Stephen Merchant, Morgan Freeman and Sanjeev Bhaskar. Who are they? Well, I never watch telly.

I tried to book an Uber home, but after all the drink I could not work my mobile. But Denise went out in the street and found a black cab and helped me into it. And she insisted on paying the taxi home. Wasn't that kind.

You, of course, would not have come with me to see the *Get Back* film, or the VIP party. If I had dragged you there, you would have turned the other way, pretending you did not see Paul. And would have been embarrassed when I went over and introduced Denise to Paul. You were always on at me for being a creep with the Beatles, which I denied then and still do.

I remember Paul staying with us in Portugal back in 1968, when he suddenly arrived with Linda. You largely ignored him, but Paul loved sitting with you late at night having intellectual talks, arguing the toss, just for the sake of it. Linda would interrupt your chat, grabbing Paul, saying, 'Come on, honey, let's go to bed...'

I did talk you into going to the *Magical Mystery Tour* private party in 1967, for the launch of the film. We all had to go in fancy dress. You and I dressed up as a Boy Scout and a Girl Guide, which was all we could think of, borrowing the clothes from neighbours. Paul and Jane Asher, then his fiancée, were dressed as a pearly king and queen. John was dressed as a Teddy boy, as he used to be, back in the fifties when he first met Paul. He had his hair swept back in a duck's arse, tight trousers and blue suede shoes.

You sat on your own by the side of the room while I went off and mingled. I came back to find that John was sitting beside you, heatedly discussing something or other. You were making him think, making him reconsider whatever daft comment or wild opinion he had just come out with. Just as you used to do with me. Nobody does that to me anymore...

Tata the noo.

LETTER SEVEN

Our wedding day, 11 June 1960.

Bypass

Heh up, it's me again.

So how has your health been these last six years, Hunt? I can hear you asking me. Still moaning about your arthritis? Got proper hearing aids yet? Nope, still not got decent ones. I did get free NHS ones and wore them for a day, then gave up. They were too uncomfortable. The family go on about it all the time. At family gatherings, I can't hear a bleeding thing, and they all shout at me. Come on, I hear you say. You can afford it! Why not spend your money? Since I am on my own quite a lot of the time – watching the telly on my own, eating on my own (oh God I will be sobbing soon and you will be scoffing...) – it's not generally a problem. But I know that eventually I will have to get a decent hearing aid. One day.

Compared with what you went through for the last forty years of your life, since your double mastectomy in 1974, my life has been a doddle. More or less. Though, hold on, there was a time not long ago when I thought I was a goner. How could I forget? But then I do tend to minimise awful things, pretend they didn't happen. Which I did with your cancer for most of the years you had it. Wiped it from my mind. Pretended it had not happened.

When I was on holiday in Portugal four years ago, early one morning I took a stroll along a clifftop, on my own, nothing strenuous. Suddenly, I felt awful chest pains, right across my body, sort of burning, stabbing, tightening. I found myself gasping for breath and had to sit down every ten yards or so. Somehow, I managed to drag myself back to our house. I thought it might be indigestion. So I had a cup of tea and a lie-down on the couch. An hour later, the pain had lifted – and I decided I would like to go for a swim in the sea, on Porto de Mós beach, which you know so well. The waves were pretty big, but I went in all the same, on my own. What an idiot. Goodness knows what might have happened while I was in the sea. But what fab times you and I had there. Antonio's caff is still there, but his son Pedro now runs it.

Next day, back in London, I thought, hmm, I had better go to my GP and tell her about my funny turn in Portugal. I hate being sensible, but when you live on your own, who else is going to be sensible for you, except yourself? I realised it was the third time in three weeks I had had these chest pains. First was on a train going to interview someone for my *London Parks* book. Next was after cutting the grass. But each time, after clutching my chest, struggling to breathe, sitting down and resting, the pain had lifted.

I did not think the pain meant much, just age, doing too much, rushing around. But I had so many events lined up, working on the new book, a trip to Carlisle, a trip to Barbados, I did not want to cancel any of them.

Then I remembered a year ago I had been in the Lake District at the wonderful Gilpin Hotel near Windermere, which has its own little lake where you can swim. Coming out of the water, I slipped on the deck, fell over and bashed my head. When I got up, I had no idea who I was, where I was, or who I was with. It was strange. I remember thinking, what a weird experience, not knowing who I am, and hoping I turn out to be someone interesting. I staggered to the hotel and asked one of the waiters where I was. And what was my name. He told me to sit down while he called the manager.

I had not been unconscious, not as far as I was aware, but clearly I had banged some part of my brain. The owner of the hotel insisted on driving me to hospital in Kendal. It took a while for me to be seen, and when I finally was, they said they couldn't do an MRI scan there. They suggested I go to the much bigger hospital in Lancaster. I ordered a taxi and I remember thinking, as we tore down the M6, oh God, the expense. Which showed I had my memory back.

The wait for an MRI was going to be three hours, so I thought bugger it, I'll just go back to the hotel. I was due in London next day and I would go first thing to A&E at the Royal Free Hospital. Which I did, and they could see nothing. In a few weeks, I had forgotten all about losing my memory – but then I started to have the chest pains.

I managed to get an emergency appointment at my GP's surgery, still the same one in Hampstead that we first joined in 1960 when we lived in the Vale of Health, but of course the doctors are all different now. Every time I go, I boast to the receptionist that I must be their longest registered patient. As if they are interested.

An emergency appointment means you get ten minutes only, and can only discuss one subject. So you can't say, 'Oh, doctor, I also have this funny rash on my bum, can you look at that as well?' I told the doctor about the chest pains. She checked my heart and immediately sent me to A&E at the Royal Free. The whole world was already ahead of me, waiting impatiently. It was Monday morning, prime time for poorly people. But eventually I was seen and started a long series of tests.

At lunchtime, a nursing assistant asked if I would like a cup of tea and a sandwich. I said thanks, lovely. She asked what sort? I said any sort, I eat anything, pet. And did she want some money for the tea and sarnie? No, she said, it was free. Isn't the NHS wonderful? She brought me a tuna and sweetcorn sandwich. Oh no, I said, making a face. Sweetcorn is about the only thing I don't really like. I hate to be a bother, but could you possibly, maybe, swap it for anything else? I'll be your best friend. She went off and came back with egg and mayonnaise. Oh God, I forgot. I also hate mayonnaise. This time I said nowt. She would quite rightly have hit with me with it if I had asked her to change it again.

I spent the next three days in a cardiology ward at the Royal Free with lots of tubes and wires, having scary-sounding tests and swallowing loads of pills. All the test results were alarming – yet I felt so fit, and such a fraud. How could there be anything wrong with me when I am so healthy, walk miles every day, swim three times a week, have never smoked, eat healthily – okay, I drink three glasses of wine a day but come on, at eighty-two my body must be used to it by now.

The first worrying test result was in A&E, where they said my cardiac enzyme levels were very elevated. What are they when they are at home? I enquired. And what is normal? Hospitals, apparently, have their own ratings. At the Royal Free, the normal level is 14, and I was... 250. I burst out laughing. I was eventually sent for an angiogram – a type of X-ray of your arteries that shows the doctors if there are blockages. If any of my arteries were blocked, they said, they would shove in some stents.

I would need an anaesthetic, but the procedure was a routine one and unlikely to be problematic. Except, of course, in the 1 per cent of cases where it goes wrong. Sign here, please. The cardiologists throw these stats around as lightly as if they were pundits on *Match of the Day* analysing the number of shots on target...

When I came round, no stents had been put in. They had

found at least six dodgy arteries – too many to fix with stents. Instead, I would have to have a triple bypass. Oh God. I ain't got time for all that. I have a book to write, don't you know? The operation would be carried out at St Bartholomew's, as the Royal Free does not do heart bypasses. I lay in the ward for another few days, while they kept an eye on me.

An Indian consultant, awfully cheerful with a lush moustache, came over from Barts to assess me. He said after the bypass I would feel ten years younger. But I don't want to be ten years younger, I said. I am quite happy being eighty-two. All I want to be is four weeks younger, before the chest pains began.

I then had a week at home, waiting for my op, amusing myself by writing postcards to friends saying I am not going to Barbados after all – I am going to St Bart's.

Do you recall years ago, one December, when I was in Venezuela researching *In Search of Columbus*, I sent you postcards datelined 'Christmas, Caracas'? Which I thought was dead witty. They took ages to arrive – most of them turned up on the day my mother died. Oh God. I was never forgiven for not being in England when she died – and for making silly jokes.

While lying in the Royal Free ward waiting to go to Barts, I was told about the worst stats to emerge from my many tests. A kindly nurse, reading my bedside medical notes, said, 'Oh goodness, your angiogram shows three of your arteries are 99%, 90% and 80% blocked!!!!' How had I survived? 'Someone is looking after you,' said several of the young docs, ever so wisely. I suppose in a way someone was looking after *you*, as you survived cancer for forty years after your mastectomy, until it returned in your spine. I know who is looking after me – you, my dear Margaret. You are my guiding star, my guardian angel. You are still looking after me, making sure I have a good and safe time, before it is full time. Then the final whistle will blow and I will join you up there. Or at least under the summerhouse.

So I had my triple bypass at Barts, reputably the best hospital in London for such operations. I felt rather privileged to be there. I remember when you had your first mastectomy at the Royal Free. You hated the butcher who did it. When a few months later you had to have the other breast done, our GP, Micky, sent you to the Marsden, the specialist cancer hospital, where you loved the surgeon, Mr McKinna. I liked him as well when I visited. You would not let the children visit. You thought they would be horrified by all the poor mutilated women in the surrounding beds.

I was the oldest person in my ward at Barts – yet I was discharged before anyone else. I was in the hospital for just five days. So I was the winner. It's pathetic, I know, but it did keep me going, help me to keep my chin up, having this competition with the others, which of course they knew nothing about. I felt pretty hellish for six weeks after I got home. I couldn't sleep. The pains in my chest were constant and I had to sleep on my back. I longed for the liquid morphine they gave me at Barts. God, that was delish. You used to love that as well, when you were in the Marie Curie hospice. Once I was discharged and at home, they would not allow me any more morphine. The GP recommended paracetamol, but I could have done with something stronger.

But I did enjoy showing the family and friends my chest scars when they came to visit. That was fun. They were so dramatic. I could not really believe they had opened up my whole chest, top to bottom, with a saw, probably a hammer and chisel as well, then sewed it up with steel wire. Meanwhile, they had messed around inside with the plumbing, bypassing the three dodgy arteries with a monster length of vein taken from my left leg. Did you know we all have veins that just lie there, doing nothing? Lazy sods.

I asked Damian, one of my surgeons, who was originally from Yorkshire, to take a photo when I was opened up, just to amuse my grandchildren. I still have it, but I don't think I can face seeing it.

Bypasses are routine these days – or so lots of kind, caring people constantly told me, thinking they were being reassuring. Routine for Barts, maybe – not for me.

Now, four years later, the scars have completely gone. When I am stripped off, or sunbathing in the back garden, which I do at the slightest glimpse of the sun, I can see no signs at all that they ever opened up my chest. Remarkable.

Poor you. Your awful operations all those years ago disfigured your chest. They had taken away so much it looked like a bomb site, with craters and scarred earth left behind forever. You refused to have any sort of reconstructive surgery, such as it was back in the 1970s. I know you were self-conscious about it for the rest of your life. You always wore your nightdress in the bedroom, all the time, but I did once by chance catch sight of you naked when you came out of the bath. I hid, so you never knew I had seen you. Afterwards, I cried. For your sake. Not mine. It honestly never worried me or turned me off you. I still loved you, as I always had done. I still wanted to cuddle you. Which eventually did happen when we got back to normal married life.

I was lucky with my bypass. The operation went well and there is no sign of it at all today. My principal emotion at the time was anger. I was angry because I did not expect it, did not see it coming; I was convinced that, drinking apart, I have led a healthy life – all that walking and swimming, and no sugar, salt or butter. And yet, because of the bypass, I lost three sodding months of my life. That was how long it took me to recover fully. At my age, losing three months means losing a big chunk of what's left of my life.

Do I fear death? I would have been well pissed off if that had been it, when I had hardly noticed there was anything wrong with me. And have I changed my ways? I asked all the medical brainboxes and the heart experts at the Royal Free and Barts what might have caused my arteries to get buggered up. They all listed the usual suspects – age, obesity, diabetes, genes. Not one of them listed alcohol as an important element. Honestly, I did ask them specially. But I did decide to cut down a bit in future. Two glasses of wine a day from now on, not three. I think that lasted about six months... Now I am back to a bottle a day, at least. It's not doing me any harm, or so I tell myself.

You always said – don't show off about your health. You are tempting fate.

One of the things I used to boast about before the heart op was that I took no pills, unlike almost all of my contemporaries. Now, since the bypass op, I have to take five pills a day for my heart. One of them is a blood thinner, which means that when I get the slightest scratch, usually without being aware of it, it bleeds for ages. A real drag. But I suppose I have to be grateful for modern medicine. I often wonder if, had you lived longer, say for another ten years, they might have found a cure for your cancer. Or simply better treatment. I do read stories of wonder cures round the corner. They are bound to come sooner or later. But you will miss them.

I am now waiting for another operation, something different. But I will save that for another letter. Don't want to spoil you. Age, eh? You don't know what is coming next. Just enjoy it while you can...

Tarrawell.

LETTER EIGHT

*Margaret and me – looking ever so smart – at
the wedding of some Oxford friends, 1960.*

Student Daze

Me again.

I have completely forgotten to tell you about all the excitements and changes in our family life, which I know you will be agog to hear.

When you hopped it back in 2016, our older granddaughters, Amelia and Ruby, were just sixteen and still at school. Now they are twenty-three and... er... I will tell you later what happened to them. Both went to university – yes, I can hardly believe it. Especially when you remember what happened to Ruby. She was a naughty one at school and was asked to leave before GSCE exams and had to find another school. Oh, the usual London comprehensive naughty stuff. Why am I saying that? Just a cheap sneer. Girls these days at private schools do just as naughty stuff. And worse, if it is a mixed school. Apparently, Ruby told a teacher to fuck off, had a bottle of vodka under her desk and pulled another girl's hair. Not quite like your own dear time at your all-girls High School in Carlisle. Hold on – that's not quite true. In those days, there was always one girl every year at school who had to leave because she was pregnant. Probably does not happen anymore. That shame has gone.

Thinking about Amelia and Ruby going to university today makes me think about you and me at that stage in our lives, back in Carlisle in the 1950s. Only 4 per cent of school-leavers went to university when I went up to Durham and you to Oxford. I was not aware of that figure till I looked it up. I had no idea I was in such a minority: at the time, it seemed the natural thing to do; it was what all our friends at school in Carlisle were doing. Today, the figure is nearer 50 per cent. And yet I don't actually remember applying to any university. When my family had moved from Scotland to Carlisle a few years previously, I was initially sent to a local secondary technical school. I didn't arrive at Carlisle Grammar School until later, when I was sixteen. I then had to do 'O' level Latin in just nine months, as I was told that no half-decent 'varsity' – yes, that was the term – would let you do an arts degree without Latin. The Latin teacher taught me and two other boys in a store cupboard during his free periods. We all passed. Wasn't that kind?

One day, the school said they were sending a group of us to Durham for interview, and I should go. All I can remember was the admissions tutor playing opera all through my interview. I passed my three 'A' levels, with a B in each, and in the autumn of 1954 I started at University College, Durham.

Durham, then and now, is residential and collegiate, but there were only nine colleges in 1954 with a total of 1,500 students. Now they have about 20,000 students in all. My college was housed in a medieval castle and I was overawed and confused by the grandeur of it all. We wore gowns, had formal dinner in Hall, maids served us, High Table had a butler, a Latin grace was said, bedders did our rooms. There was a buttery that served food and drink, such as sherry, from bottles with the college crest on. You didn't pay cash; you signed a chit and it went on your 'battels', as termly bills are called at certain colleges at Durham (and also at Oxford, I believe). When you were in your room, you 'sported your Oak' (i.e. your external wooden door) to show you were working or were busy trying to persuade a girl to lie on the bed. Some chance. Sex was not invented till 1963. Anyway, I had you as my girlfriend back home in Carlisle.

We both grew up on the same sort of council estate, with parents who had left school at thirteen. But, unlike me, you were always brilliant at school. Oh yes you were. Your school was so proud of you when you got your open scholarships. Your name went up on the honours board in the hall at the Carlisle and County High School for Girls. The school does not physically exist anymore. I wonder where the honours board went.

When you went to Somerville, I used to hitchhike from Durham to see you. Remember that afternoon we somehow fell asleep in your room and woke up to find it was eight o'clock – by which time all the male visitors had to be out. The rules were even stricter at Durham. At one of the women's colleges, St Mary's, girls had to push their bed into the corridor when entertaining a man. With your help, I decided to escape from Somerville disguised as a woman – wearing your raincoat, college scarf round my head and my trousers pulled up. You did not realise then how naff it was to wear a college scarf, being fresh out of Carlisle. I strode boldly through the porter's lodge, said 'good night' in a high-pitched voice, then ducked into an alley and started rolling down my trouser legs. I had noticed a couple kissing good night who were watching me. I was not aware he was the editor of the Oxford University student newspaper, *Cherwell*. He ran a story about a man escaping from Somerville dressed as a woman. Someone then sneaked on you and gave your name to *Cherwell*, who flogged the story to Fleet Street, to the *Daily Sketch*. You were gated, bringing the good name of the college into disrepute. Disgusting.

I absolutely loved Durham, though I spent most of my first year drinking, playing shove ha'penny, messing about, with no idea what I was going to do in life. Teach, probably, to please my mum. By chance, I started writing funny pieces for *Palatinate*, the student newspaper. I had been to a Boat Club dinner in Castle Hall, got drunk and thrown an orange at a friend on another table, which missed him and hit a medieval stained-glass window. I hid under the table. The first piece I wrote was about this event, the diary of a Boat Club Hearty, full of bad spelling. 'Gorrup was sic out of the winder, had brakefast, bak to my rume, was sick out winder.'

I eventually became editor of *Palatinate* and was also, boast boast, Senior Man of my college, which meant president of our junior common room. Oh, I was such a hack. That was the phrase then. You never liked Oxford, or so you said. You found the history course boring, felt your creativity was being knocked out of you. You used to say you would have learned more about life if you had gone into Carr's biscuit works in Carlisle as a cracker packer. I think that was partly a tease, to annoy the dons. Yet, despite rubbishing Oxford, you did for a while, with my prompting, give it a go, and joined in student life. I was loving it so much at Durham I was always telling you to try new activities, to see if you liked them. It wouldn't matter if you gave them up quickly.

You did follow my example for a while and did some journalism, becoming film critic of the student magazine *Isis*. You also wrote a feature for *Isis* saying why you much preferred reading *Woman's Own* to the *Guardian*. That led to an invite from *Woman's Own* to come to London and have lunch at the Guards Club. I was so jealous. Nobody from Fleet Street ever wrote to me at Durham. I worried, of course, that there might be some hanky-panky in the taxi on the way to the Guards Club. You did have the lunch, but turned down their job offers.

When we went to university, back in the fifties, everything was paid for. We could not have gone otherwise. And not just tuition fees and accommodation: they even paid our train fares from Carlisle each term. When you graduated in 1960 – the same year we got married – you still had £100 left from your scholarships. I immediately helped you spend it.

You never went back to Oxford in your whole life. When your books began to do well, Somerville offered you an honorary fellowship. I found the letter in the drawer in your office after you died. It said you would get a free room any time you were in Oxford and dinner at High Table. I remember saying: 'Great, I will come with you.' But you said: 'Why would I want that? I am never going back to Oxford.' So you turned it down. Foony woman.

When each of our three children in turn reached the age of eighteen, you put no pressure on them to try for university. Unlike me. 'Oh, you'll love it,' I kept on telling them, 'the best time I ever had, you'll discover things you never knew you could do, meet people you would not otherwise have met.' Caitlin went to Sussex and did American Studies. On our visits, I used to nag her to write for the student newspaper. I knew she could write (and today she is the author of twelve books) but she refused. 'Okay then,' I said, 'why not do stuff for the campus radio station, you have a lovely voice, oh yes you have.' Nope, she joined nowt.

When Jake went to Cambridge, to Caius College, and did History, I don't remember him joining anything either, though various awful-sounding exclusive societies invited him to be a member. He did captain the college football team, though. And made his old dad proud.

I suppose I drove both of them mad with my pushy ways, wanting them to join things, going on about the wonders of university life, how I loved Durham, best time of my life, blah blah, a time when everything opened up for me. You, on the other hand, never raved about Oxford.

Flora, when her turn came, despite getting two As at 'A' level, refused to go to university. At the time, she saw her older siblings with their excellent arts degrees doing nothing very much apart from travelling abroad. Instead, she wanted to learn something useful. So she went to art college, to the London College of Printing, and studied screen printing. She lived either at home or in a flat nearby. So she was never a student, in the going-away sense. I only remember visiting her college once, for her final-year exhibition.

By this time, in the 1980s and 90s, university tuition was still free, but you now had to pay for accommodation and maintenance. Going to visit Caitlin at Sussex was my first experience of a new university, on a purpose-built campus, unlike Durham and Oxford. When she first arrived, Caitlin lived on the campus at Falmer – and hated it. She didn't like being surrounded by students who were all the same age as her – exactly what you used to complain about at Oxford. She then moved into a room in Brighton. On our first visit, you opened the oven and a rat jumped out. Even I was appalled – and I have pretty low standards. So we decided to buy a flat in a Regency house in Bedford Square, near the West Pier. Since we were paying for her accommodation anyway, it seemed to make sense. She shared the flat with another girl, who paid rent, which became Caitlin's maintenance. At the time (the 1980s), I had never heard of any other parents forking out on a flat for their children to live in while they were at university – it even seemed a bit flash – but it is now quite common practice in well-off middle-class families. With ever-increasing house prices, and student numbers always going up, you can double what you paid for a flat for your little darling in five years. And that's exactly what I did, after Caitlin finally left Sussex.

Jake's Cambridge college was of course ancient and architecturally stunning, with a fabulous quad (whoops, sorry, I forgot: quadrangles are called 'courts' in Cambridge lingo), but I can't now remember him living in the really old parts. He was for a while in a modern wing, a bit like Falmer at Sussex – not nearly as grand as my set of rooms in the Norman Gallery in Durham Castle when I was Senior Man. As I was always telling him.

Must have a rest now, as I always do after lunch, especially after a few drinks. When I get back, I will bring you up to date on our two older grandchildren and university education today. Stand by your bed. Do you have beds in Heaven? Or do you just sleep on clouds?

Zzzzzzzz.

LETTER NINE

Margaret with… George Best? Hold on a minute – it's me.
Back in Carlisle somewhere, looking very sixties.

Granddaughters

Hi again, pet, if you are still there. It's me again, back after my rest.

Ruby managed to get into a sixth-form college and sat her 'A' levels and got into Essex to read – wait for it – law. Amazing. So enterprising of her. My granddaughter the lawyer, I kept telling the neighbours. Almost as worth boasting about as my son the barrister. Amelia, always a good girl at school, got into Leeds to read English, but I think she really hankered after doing something arty in TV or design or painting.

While they were still at their respective unis – as we have to call them today – I went to see them both, each aged twenty and in their second years of study at places and institutions I know nothing about. It was like visiting a strange, overpopulated, exotic foreign country with its own language. In some ways it took me back to when you and I were at university almost seventy years ago, and thirty years ago to our own children's university years – but dear God, the changes that have happened in education in our recent lifetime.

Before setting off, I vowed to myself I would not drive them potty by going on about how I adored Durham, what you should do, pet, back in my day, etc.

First of all, I went to visit Ruby at Essex. I had heard of the University of Essex, and that it was good for politics and social studies, but I did not know where it actually was. Was it in a town, or out in the wilds – and if so, where? It turned out to be a couple of miles outside Colchester, one of the oldest towns in all England, built by the Romans, but I had to get off the train at a place nearby called Hythe, where I was met by Ruby. She looked glamorous and healthy, smiley and cheerful, considering it must have been such a drag for her to get up so early to meet me. (It came out later that, unless she had a 9.30 lecture, she slept till two o'clock. Students, eh?) It was a ten-minute walk to where she lived, through a nondescript industrial wasteland, filled with factories and workshops, which could have been in any area of urban England today.

She was living in a new, purpose-built block, privately built and owned, lived in by students. Yet the block looked too smart and affluent for students, more like a superior Premier Inn. There was a gated entrance and lots of pressing of buttons. Inside, there was a reception desk, some security person lurking in the background, a coffee machine, TV room, a gym, all new and immaculate. No sign of graffiti anywhere. Two Chinese boys were playing billiards, but otherwise there was not much sign of human life.

We went down a corridor and she opened her door. 'I hope it doesn't smell,' she said. She had just left it twenty minutes ago, so I wondered how it would smell. 'Oh, rooms do have a smell,' said Ruby, 'when you come in from outside.' It smelled fine to me, not the sweaty-socks smell that is my memory of my student rooms. But then Ruby is an ace cleaner. In your last few years, when you were really ill, you employed Ruby as a cleaner and you said she was brilliant.

Ruby's room was a large studio flat, amazingly well equipped with a double bed, her own kitchen, WC and shower, fridge-freezer and giant TV. Every student in the block has a 40-inch Samsung TV, which comes with the room and does not cost any extra. Samsung is apparently one of the sponsors of the block. Her flat was quite expensive, £190 a week, in what is considered a luxury block by student standards. In one of the high-rise tower blocks right on the campus, her room would be cheaper and smaller. Further down the corridor, she said, there were deluxe flats at £250 a week, popular with wealthier foreign students. She took me to see one, where an Indian friend of hers lives, but he wasn't in. Or was asleep. Or not answering.

It was a thirty-minute walk to the campus, but she said she could phone for a minicab for us – I would probably not want to walk all that way. Cheeky sod. As we stood at the gates waiting, two other minicabs arrived, bringing food. The well-off foreign students get food sent from Waitrose. Ruby buys hers from Tesco.

The University of Essex has one of the largest proportions of foreign students of any English university – one-third of the 15,000 total come from abroad. They tend to be well-off sons and daughters of politicians and successful businesspeople. 'But they are all very humble,' Ruby tells me. 'They live just like the rest of us, do the same things. It's only if they talk about their life at home, back in Dubai or Hong Kong or wherever, and mention their cars and servants, that you realise how different their backgrounds are. If they fail an exam or don't turn up to lectures, they have it harder than British students. They are threatened with having their visas taken away, told they are not being serious with their studies, and will have to leave.' 'But I thought today's universities depended on them, as they pay so much more in fees?' I said. 'You would have thought so,' Ruby replied. 'It doesn't make sense. I think it is because British students have a better support system.'

The vast majority of the British students at Essex are from state schools, like Ruby. She was yet to meet anyone who went to a private school. But many, many of the foreign students are pretty pukka. One of her friends is related to the Queen of Spain and another to a Saudi prince.

The University of Essex was established in 1963 on a greenfield site, 200 acres of what was Wivenhoe Park. Its alumni include John Bercow, the ex-Speaker of the House of Commons, the former Tory cabinet minister Virginia Bottomley and the film director Mike Leigh. It boasts five Nobel Prize winners – who either studied at Essex or were on the staff. The university normally comes somewhere in the top thirty in the national rankings, and usually in the top five for social sciences. I do hope you are making notes. In 2018, it was named university of the year by *The Times Higher Education Supplement*. There are still signs on the campus saying 'University of the Year' – not revealing which year, of course – to impress parents and applicants.

The campus is like a small town, with shops, bars, gyms, lots of brutal-looking student residential blocks, but a nice lake and fountain. The most attractive buildings are the academic ones, such as the Business School. One was filled with palm trees, so I took photos of Ruby and told Caitlin I was in the tropics with her daughter.

We went to the student bar, which was large and comfortable, doing meals as well as drinks, and with a large TV screen for the football. It seemed to be the busiest place on the campus, even though it was only mid-morning. Earlier in the term, Ruby got herself banned from the student bar for a short while. Details were never revealed, or at least were hidden from me, her old grandad. I told her how I got drunk at a Boat Club dinner at Durham. So what happened to you, my sweet? 'Oh, it was stupid. They ban you for nothing. If you take drinks in from outside, you get banned. If you vomit, they fine you £10.' Oh Ruby, that is so unfair. So what happened? 'I didn't punch anybody. I just told one of the staff to piss off.'

We then moved on to pleasanter things – her course. She was studying law with philosophy for an LLB. In her first-year exams, she got a first in philosophy and an upper second in law. Her plan is to be a lawyer specialising in IP. Come on, you must know what that is – intellectual property. She normally has four lectures a week, lasting two hours. There can be up to two hundred students in the hall for the law lectures, as it is very popular at Essex. They are purely instructional, no questions, just listening, though you can always watch again later on a video. For the philosophy bit of her course, she has a tutorial once a week, often with only four other students.

'I have a lot of essays and also set work, which you have to read for and prepare and write 500 words – then it gets discussed.'

Alas, despite my vow, over lunch I found myself nagging Ruby about not joining things, as I had done with her mother. I suggested the debating society – must be one – as she is so fluent and good at arguing. At your funeral in 2016, she stood up without notes and gave a touching speech. 'The only thing I have thought about is first aid – as it's a practical skill. And I'd like to do some swimming, but I haven't found a pool yet. I might join the Afro-Caribbean society, but I've not got round to it.' I suppose this might be vaguely connected to the fact that Ruby's father – from whom her mother is long divorced – is from Botswana, where Ruby was born. He was at one time an MP in Botswana.

She said she is loving the course, but that life on the campus was a bit boring, as there is not a lot to do when you're not working. 'The drinking culture is very strong, but I don't want to get involved in that. The various nationalities tend to stick together socially. It's the Brits who do all the drinking.'

The university has a tradition of political protest, but on

the day of my visit it was all quiet and calm. I stopped at a stall run by the Islamic Society. They turned out to be selling mosque rugs, only £3 each. I bought one. What a bargain.

Ruby has a little job, cleaning once a week for two of the better-off students. She gets paid between £25 and £30 for two hours' work. Students never had jobs in my day, not during term time. We didn't need to work as most aspects of our student lives were already paid for.

Amelia, daughter of Jake and Rosa, was also in her second year – at Leeds, studying English and Film Studies. I had not been to Leeds for years and was surprised how glossy and modern it all seemed – and goodness, with so many students. In my day, there was just one university in Leeds: now there are four – the University of Leeds, Leeds Beckett (formerly Leeds Metropolitan), Leeds Trinity and Leeds Arts, plus several more colleges and other educational establishments. There must be 80,000 students in Leeds. Leeds University itself has 33,000 students and is considered one of the top universities in England, a member of the Russell Group. There did not seem to be as many overseas students as at Essex. Most of the accents I heard sounded southern and middle-class. When I was at Durham in the fifties, almost everyone seemed to be like me – from a northern grammar school. The southerners were the foreigners. Amelia agreed Leeds was very southern, but she personally did not know many students from private schools, it's just that the affluent middle classes go to great lengths to hide any signs of wealth.

I asked if many arrived with chips on their shoulders not having got into Oxbridge, which was common at Durham in the 1950s. She thought the opposite. 'They think Leeds is cool and Oxford old-fashioned.'

That year, she was living in a private house about half an hour from the campus with five other girls. They have a bedroom each and, like Ruby, she has a spacious double bed. I only had a horrible single bed at Durham, with an army surplus blanket. It was like camping. I remember your bed at Oxford being equally small. Amelia shared a living room and kitchen, neither of which she would let me enter. She said they were both tips. But she had tidied her bedroom for my arrival. It was large and attractive, with a window looking onto the street. The room was full of evidence of Amelia's design talent. Well, her mother did go to St Martin's and is now a set designer. So it's in her genes.

Amelia had a slight wobble in her first year when she got bored by her English course, which was all eighteenth-century. She thought of leaving university and going to art college. In seminars, there is interaction with the lecturers, which Amelia usually takes part in. 'Some people don't like talking in front of others, but I don't mind. I hate silence, so I try to fill it.' She says she is working hard and will try to get a first-class degree (following in her daddy's footsteps). Like Ruby, Amelia had not joined any student societies, but she did plenty of other stuff outside her academic coursework. She did illustrations for a student magazine called *Lippy* and spent one day a week in a social media start-up firm, helping with their visuals. She didn't get paid, but it will look good on her CV. She was also making some money designing T-shirts. She produced one showing caricatures of her friends, and they all wanted one. She uses a firm called Everpress, who make and market them. She receives up to £5 for each T-shirt sold.

Like all students today – well, all students at all times – there was a lot of drinking. Amelia admitted she got pretty hammered most weekends. Girls today do tend to do it even more than the boys. Unlike Ruby, she had not been banned from the student bar. In fact, she hardly ever goes there. They start drinking in town, then go back to a student house. I said I felt sorry for their landlords. She said theirs is fine. He will always come if there are problems, like needing to call a plumber or someone to mend the electrics.

The cost of it all is the biggest single change since we were at university, of course. I reckon a student today has somehow to find around £9,000–£20,000 for fees, £7,000 for accommodation and £4,000 for living expenses. Not like in our day, when everything was totally free. Or have I already said that? Students can of course sleep together, all the time – so that is a big plus. That would have been our ultimate fantasy in the 1950s. No need today to put the bed in the corridor…

So how did things work out for Amelia and Ruby? They graduated with good 2:1s last year, both of them I think a bit disappointed they did not get firsts. Ruby has now started at the University of Law in London, studying for her professional qualifications to be a solicitor. It will take time, as she failed a couple of her exams. The system today with solicitors and accountants is that in your postgraduate year, normally while working, you have to plough through loads of mind-boggling stuff, but if you fail any parts, you are allowed several other goes to resit. To earn money to live on as she completes her legal studies, Ruby has been working hard as a dog walker.

Amelia has also shown enterprise by working, not lolling around doing nothing. For six months, she worked in a hamburger joint near Oxford Street. Now she has a proper staff job, as a production assistant at an events company. And she finds the time to manage a musician on a freelance basis as well. So are the careers of our older grandchildren sorted? Will one become Solicitor General and the other a Famous Film Director? Does it matter, as long as they are happy, don't frighten the horses and are always kind to their old grandad, bringing him a glass of Sauvignon Blanc, even when he hasn't asked for one?

Who knows what will happen to them? Or to me. But watch this space. Will try to keep you up to date. Bye for now…

LETTER TEN

On the set of Georgy Girl, *1966. Margaret with two of the
stars of the film, Lynn Redgrave and James Mason.*

Family Matters

Hiya, pet, it's me again.

So what about the rest of the family? Caitlin is the only one who has experienced an upheaval in her life – fortunately, not a professional or marital one. She's gone and moved out of London to another place. A bit potty, I think, which she hates me saying, so don't tell her I said so.

The other two are still in the same north London houses they were living in when you moved on to your new abode.

Jake is just a ten-minute walk away from me. Which is handy, now that I have started falling and fading. Jake and Rosa have the whole house, apart from a lodger in the basement flat, as Amelia moved into her own little flat after she started work. Jake is still a barrister, doing employment law. Rosa is still working in the theatre as a set designer; she has mostly been doing experimental productions, but now appears to be having a golden spell, doing a Royal Shakespeare Company show. The big recent excitement in their life is that they have a new dog called Lilo, who is – oh I forget, having no interest in dogs – some sort of Border collie cross. Coco, their springer spaniel, whom you will remember, died a year ago and they were in mourning for a month.

Flora is still living on the Harringay Ladder. When you look at her local streets around Green Lanes, they do run like a ladder. We thought they were slumming it when they first moved there, but the area has come up in the world, and she has had MPs and lawyers as neighbours. Richard had an awful motorcycle accident a few years ago, while coming home late at night on his motorbike from his job at the time, managing a smart restaurant in Chelsea. He was injured for months, had to have a steel rod put in his arm and could not work, but he has made a full recovery. He is now working from home, running his own recruitment company. Which seems to be going well as he has just taken on an assistant.

Flora returned to her art, refusing to go back to TV production, which she did for some years, becoming a producer, and is getting lots of work with her designs. I could send you a link to her website, which is most impressive, but you always were rubbish at anything technical. You never even managed to type, and yet you were a writer all your life.

Their two girls, Amarisse and Sienna, are at a local girls' comprehensive in Hornsey. So grown-up and mature, they look twenty-four and twenty-five, not fourteen and fifteen. Sienna is passionate about football, plays for a local women's team and trains most evenings. Poor Flora has to drive her to training, which is often miles away. While she's waiting for Sienna to finish, she inspects all the charity shops, garden centres, nurseries and supermarkets in the area. Amarisse is tall and ever so glamorous and has a big following for her blog, which mainly seems to be about her latest hairstyle. Modern gels, eh?

Caitlin is still with Nigel, still writing lots of books, all of them excellent, in my humble opinion. Do you remember her lovely book about the four swimming ponds on Hampstead Heath? She gets published by good publishers, but they tend to be niche books and don't sell much. Typical of all publishing these days, unless you are a bestseller or a celeb. In our day, when we were starting, things were easier, publishers stood by you and were not too worried about specialised or unusual subjects. She has had TV and film rights sold but not yet been made, such as her book about Holloway Prison, which you would have loved and been most impressed by.

Remember how rude you were to me when you were writing *Significant Sisters* all those years ago, your book about women who changed the lives of other women? That Christmas, I got you what I thought was a really brilliant present – the autographs of the three Pankhursts. You looked at them and sniffed, 'What are these? I have no interest in autographs. There is no content in signature...' I was furious, but, having got the Pankhursts, I started collecting suffragette material myself. I probably still have about a thousand items. Just one of my twenty collections in my room, which you used to moan about, saying they were just collecting dust. 'If you go first,' you used to say, 'it will be straight to the dump.' Meaning all my collections, not my body, I hope.

I have never written about my suffragette material or turned it into a book. But when Caitlin was doing her Holloway Prison book, I was able to give her some suffragette letters. So there. My collection did turn out useful after all.

Caitlin has moved from London to the seaside. It had always been her fantasy, to live by the sea, and now she is living it. Being a writer, she can live anywhere and so can her partner, Nigel, who works at home for an online newspaper, doing the layout. You will remember when they met twenty years ago he was a photographer.

At first, they moved into the house in Broadstairs that the children had bought with the money I got from selling our house in Loweswater in 2016. But didn't I tell you that earlier? Do concentrate.

Broadstairs is a handsome seaside town. I like the fact that when you come out of the station, you are at the end of the main street and can immediately look straight ahead and see the sea. In the neighbouring towns of Margate and Ramsgate, the station is not as handily situated, nor as attractive. Broadstairs has a strong connection with Charles Dickens, who spent many holidays here. There's a Bleak House on the cliff (where he wrote *David Copperfield*) and a pub and a house named after him. It is now open to the public as a museum.

The cottage the children bought is outside Broadstairs, overlooking a lovely quiet bay. It's not built up at all, unlike the main bay in Broadstairs, Viking Bay, which is very attractive, but gets busy in the summer, hoaching with trippers down from London. Our bay is always empty, except for one small caff plus lifeguards in the season and a long row of beach huts, all artistically painted. There are chalk cliffs all the way along, but the beach is broad and you can walk out and along it for miles when the tide is out. The drag for me has always been getting down to the beach from our cottage. You have to go down some steep steps, cut through the cliff – it's very dramatic, when you suddenly spot the sea at last – but my poor old legs are not up to all the steps, more than a hundred of them. I counted them with Amarisse and Sienna when they were younger, but I've now forgotten exactly how many.

Caitlin and Nigel lived there for about six months, but they have moved away and bought their own seaside house on a different part of the coast. I have not seen it yet, but I will be visiting soon. Can't wait. But I will have to button my lip. Apparently, it is a bungalow. A bungalow! Aren't they for old people? I will have to say nowt.

Caitlin wants to be near the sea as she does wild-water swimming most of the year round, and has written three books about it. She had thought that when she got to sixty, that was when she would move to the seaside. She has just done it a couple of years earlier than she had planned. Sixty! Our little daughter will be sixty in 2024. I can't believe it. I can still see myself visiting her on the day she was born in the maternity hospital in Hampstead, though I missed her actual birth. I got fed up waiting for you to give birth, so I went off to buy a pork pie and when I got back, Caitlin had arrived.

Even more amazing, Flora has just turned fifty on Hallowe'en... Flora, our baby. Can you believe it? It makes me feel a hundred. Which I suppose I nearly am.

As for me, despite having the Isle of Wight cottage as my own holiday home, I am still in our old London house beside the Heath, which you and I moved into in 1963. I had a party recently to celebrate sixty years in this house. I am now the longest resident of our street, since the Gladstones moved out and downsized into a flat. Did I tell you I now have three summerhouses? I don't have a car anymore, so the garage has been converted into a garden room. It looks lovely, cool and artistic.

More recently, I have added a very attractive and expensive conservatory to the dining room. The children thought I was mad, losing a bit of the courtyard. My theory is that when I am old, much older than I am today, and can't manage the stairs, I will have retreated downstairs and will be living full time on the ground floor. The conservatory will be my summer bedroom. My winter bedroom will be in the living room, where you once slept for three months, after one of your operations.

I hope I will still have Denise as my lodger on the top floor, or some other lodger, paying a modest rent. On the middle floor, in our old bedroom, I will probably install some sort of paid carer, to mop my brow, give me my medications, change my nappy or whatever. I am determined not to move out of this house into a home, if I can avoid it. But all old people say that.

They say they want to die in their own bed. Being realistic, I am sure that, like you, I will spend my last days in a hospice. When you need medical care and attention round the clock, a hospice is clearly the best way. I know you believed assisted suicide should be an option for those suffering from painful, terminal illnesses, and contributed for years to a charity that campaigned for it – I've forgotten the name, it begins with a D – and planned to catch a train to Switzerland when the time came, but you never did. You weren't fit enough to travel. I am sure that happens to lots of people with similar plans.

Oh, Tortee, the tortoise. I nearly forgot her. I mean him. He is alive and well. Sleeping at this moment, as I write, having dug himself down six inches under, somewhere in the earth under the foliage against the brick wall, as he has done for fifty-five years. Yes, he is a bloke. After all these years referring to Tortee as a she, it turns out he is a he. Very fashionable today, having a gender change. (Hope there is no one up in Heaven censoring these letters who might think I am making fun of gender reassignment.)

It was during the amazingly tropical summer we had a year ago, in 2022, temperatures up to 100 in old money... I was rubbing her nose one day, about to give her a treat of some rotten tomatoes, when suddenly, blow me, between her back legs popped out what was clearly a little willy. All these years we never noticed. Perhaps it was too cold for it to venture out. Or do they need tropical weather to get excited?

Later that summer, I began to notice that he was sitting in the back yard over a crack in the York stone paving slabs, beautifully put down by Mick with his dog ten years ago. As you will remember. We were both thrilled by the good job he did. Then one morning I noticed a pool of what I thought was milk on the York stones. Where could that have come from? It is only me in this house, well mostly, and I don't remember spilling any milk. I realised it must have been Tortee, playing with himself on the cracks. Well, we all have to have our fun. Even people who live on their own. He is, after all, only thirty years younger than me. And at eighty-six this year, I am still having fun. Or trying to have fun, hoping to have fun…

More about fun in a later epistle. Under a plain wrapper, of course. Don't want to upset any sensitive souls in Heaven…

LETTER ELEVEN

Portugal, 1968. A bearded Paul McCartney with his new girlfriend Linda and her daughter Heather, plus Jake (with me) and Caitlin (with Margaret). Note Margaret's Vidal Sassoon hairdo and Mary Quant dress.

We Do Like to Be Beside the Seaside

Hi, pet, stand by your bed for more family updates and family seaside memories.

I've just been to stay with Caitlin and Nigel in their new seaside house. I don't think you and I ever stayed with our children over the years. As grown-ups, they have mainly lived so near us, in London, that there was no need. You would feel a bit spare anyway, as a parent, staying with them. They are still your children, albeit grown up, so you want to boss them around, tell them not to do that, do it this way, don't you know I don't take sugar. But if it is their house, being run and organised their way, you would have to hold back.

Hmm, that's not all correct. How could I forget? Must be age. When Caitlin lived in Botswana for fifteen years, when she was married to Ron, we used to go out every second year and stay with them in Maun, the town where they lived, out in the bush. Do you remember the dramatic sight of all those waters flooding into the Okavango Delta? Suddenly, there were rivers and lakes all around us and crocodiles and hippos sliding and slithering about in front of our eyes, watching us menacingly.

Any seaside holiday, almost anywhere, is lovely, especially with your family. Weren't those early years in Portugal wonderful, when we first bought that little house at Porto de Mós, on a cliff, with fab views all the way down the coast to

Sagres, the Land's End of Europe? When the children were young, they used to run down the cliff path every morning, ever so excited, for a day on the beach. Then in the evening I would grill sardines outside in our cobbled courtyard. It took me hours, as I could never light the charcoal. The smoke was awful – everyone got bored and fed up waiting for me to cook the damn things.

We had a routine on the beach, when Caitlin and Jake were young, around six and four, before Flora was born. We took turns, half an hour each, at sitting on our own and sunbathing or swimming, then spent half an hour trying to amuse the children. You were more quiet and sensible with them. I tended to rev them up when it was my turn.

When I first met you, you used to rave about your childhood seaside trips to Silloth on the Solway. My parents never took me there. They were strangers to Carlisle and to England, having grown up and lived around Glasgow, so I did not inherit the same family traditions as you did. They had never heard of Silloth and did not know the train went there, or where Carlisle station was. You wrote somewhere about your excitement going on the train on a Saturday from Carlisle with your sister and parents, just as their own parents had done when they were small. The whole train was always packed with families going for a day out, for 'a bit of a blow'. That was the phrase, as Silloth-on-Solway could be a bit windy. In those days, working-class families did not go abroad, or fly on a plane. Or eat avocado. Many years later, when your parents died, you paid for a memorial chair on Silloth Green, in their memory, as they loved it so much. Last year, someone in Carlisle, whom I did not know, sent me a photo of your bench in memory of Lily and Arthur, lying wrecked. It had either been vandalised or more likely fallen to pieces. The council was supposed to have looked after it, but of course councils have no money these days.

The writer of the letter had noticed there was a plaque on the derelict seat and asked if I would like him to rescue it and post it to me. Which he did. I sent him one of my Lakeland books as a thank-you. I am so kind. I have the plaque in front of me now.

IN MEMORY OF LILIAN 1901–1981
and
ARTHUR G. FORSTER 1900–1996
WHO LOVED SILLOTH

I have not yet decided where to put it. Perhaps in the summerhouse where half your ashes are buried? I already have another plaque in the garden, which you created, which I have fixed to a wooden bench. Just as it used to be in our Loweswater garden. Do you remember it? It was for our golden wedding anniversary, I think. No, hold on. I will go out and look at it now. Sorry, our ruby wedding. You were always better than me at dates and anniversaries.

11 JUNE 2000
HAPPY RUBY ANNIVERSARY HUNTER
FROM YOUR LUCKY WIFE

Some of your old girl friends on first reading the wording were appalled. It was the phrase 'from your lucky wife' that upset them. They always considered you an independent woman, a feminist, just as they were, and so could not believe that you had written something so apparently craven and off-message. They always say that it was me who was the lucky one. You looked after me all our married life, and the house and the cooking and cleaning and the children. I never did anything domestic. Back in 2000, when I told you about their reaction on first seeing the plaque, you just laughed. Said it was partly a joke.

Over the thirty summers we spent in Loweswater, we always had one trip to the seaside at Silloth, parking near the Green, then walking to Grune Point and round. It's still one of my favourite walks – always so empty and atmospheric. On every walk you reminisced how, when you were at school, aged about sixteen, you and two other girls went camping here on the Solway grass dunes. Such fun you had, so you said. I don't think parents would allow their teenage daughter such freedom today.

Over the years, other seaside holidays featured large in our married life. I suppose the most amazing one, which I still go on about, was the famous trip we did for my fiftieth birthday in 1986 – when I booked us on Concorde to fly to Barbados. Well, famous in our family legends anyway. I have rather gone off Barbados in the years since. Instead of plantations growing bananas and sugar like when we first went, all they seem to grow now is golf courses and villas. We went on to fall in love with a much smaller, unspoiled island, Bequia in the Grenadines. I am dying to go there again, visit our old haunts, if only I can find some nice, sympathetic, loving person to go with me. Not much sign of that at the moment. But I live in hope.

It was handy, being a single man of a certain age, and not as fit as I was, to be able to go and spend a few days at the seaside with some of the children at their Broadstairs cottage. And now I can visit Caitlin and Nigel at their new place, in a seaside town I had never visited before.

You would love the Isle of Wight. As I said, I have kept on the house there. I am making occasional visits on my own, while I decide what to do. In fact, I wrote a book about my first year on the island. I'll send you a copy. I bet you can hardly wait! When I first arrived on the island three years ago, I was told it was like Carlisle in the fifties. That's not quite true, but it does have a slower pace of life than the mainland.

My house there is Grade II listed – posh, eh? – just three minutes from a flat sandy beach. You can walk along it for about five miles. I love it dearly, even though I stay there on my own and have to trail there on my own – on the bus, Tube, train, then hovercraft across the Solent. I got rid of the car after you died. One of the best things I have done since you departed.

Caitlin's new house by the seaside turned out to be a period bungalow, from the 1930s, with lovely stained glass, big picture windows and a little sloping garden at the front, which made it look taller and bigger and more interesting than an ordinary bungalow. The street itself is pretty suburban, with the sort of neat pre-war houses you see in all English seaside towns – retirement homes for hard-working respectable couples from the towns – but Caitlin's bungalow is right at the end of the street, near the sea and restaurants and shops.

The internal arrangement is interesting. You enter into a large dining–sitting room, from which all the other rooms radiate. I kept getting lost, forgetting which door led to my bedroom.

Caitlin has her own office, a well-built shed in her back courtyard, where she goes each morning at six and starts writing. Yes, six in the morning. I feel sorry for Nigel, having a partner who gets up so early.

Caitlin mainly writes non-fiction these days – her most recent book was about women private eyes. She wants to return to fiction, but it is so hard to get commissioned. I am so glad that one of our children is a writer. It means that we can moan about the same things and rubbish agents and publishers. When Jake the barrister talks about his work, I don't understand what he actually does. Apart from her book writing, Caitlin is also a Royal Literary Fund Fellow and has worked in various places, such as the University of Westminster, the Science Museum and the V&A. Just a day or two a week. She is currently with a local hospital near where she now lives. Hospital staff, from porters to consultants, can make an appointment with her when they have something to write, from a thesis to a CV. It gives her a modest and steady income to augment her own writing career.

I had a great three days with them, just on my own of course, as I still have no partner to go places with, sob sob, and was treated like royalty – tea in bed, bacon sandwiches when I felt peckish. We went out one evening to an excellent Italian restaurant, just a few minutes away. There is also a pub nearby and a grocer's – much more convenient than the Broadstairs house, which is a long way from any shops. I can see why Caitlin chose to move there. She says she is in her bungalow for good. Who would have thought it? After all those decades as a nomad, in the USA studying or working in all those colleges, from California to New England, and of course her many years in Botswana. They do seem happy and settled.

And I did like the bungalow. I didn't have to bite my tongue after all, and I didn't let slip any catty remarks about geriatric living…

While I was with them, they were planning to invite all the family down for the annual Davies family Christmas lunch. Miles ahead, but, as you may remember, Caitlin, like me, is a great organiser, always making arrangements and lists. Yes, we have retained the tradition of all the family having Christmas dinner together – all eleven of us. (Three children, three partners, four granddaughters and me.)

In the old days, you of course always made Christmas dinner for the whole family, usually plus extra relations and friends. Since then, we have had the same sort of gathering, but taking it in turns to have it at our respective houses. I did it three years ago – and it was a big success. No really, I cooked everything on my own, apart from the salads, which they brought. They were most complimentary. And amazed.

You will be amused to hear that one minor tradition has also been preserved – the family Christmas quiz. I did it for decades, with prizes – usually rubbish presents left over from the year before. Then, for many years, Caitlin took over the role of quizmaster. Now Amarisse does it each year. Whoever does it makes sure there is at least one question about each of the eleven family members, about what they have been doing in the previous year. I also still insist on my Predictions. As you know, these began back in 1964 when you and I sat down on New Year's Eve, just the two of us, and tried to predict what would happen in the year ahead – such as would our first baby be a boy or a girl. We did not know the answer till March 1964, when Caitlin arrived. We always predict nice things, and still do, such as good exam results if someone in the family is sitting them, or fab reviews if one of us has a book coming out. Never sad or negative things.

I think the grown-ups are now a bit bored by it, and tire of it quickly, but Amarisse and Sienna still enjoy doing it. We always begin with me reading out the Predictions and Concerns from the previous year, and we all jeer at what we got wrong or laugh at the petty worries – the leaking roofs and bad backs – we now can't remember worrying about. I have kept all these family predictions in a folder, going back to 1964. Will they be chucked out when I am gone? Will anyone be interested? I hope Caitlin – the only collector in the family, apart from me – will preserve them. I do like these family traditions. Such fun. And I do hope they will carry on long after me.

And I hope I can make the annual family gathering this coming Christmas. It will be the first time we have held it at the seaside. And, of course, I do so wish you could join us. But at least you now know roughly what will happen and where it will take place.

Toodle pip.

LETTER TWELVE

*Margaret in London. I think someone else
had had the pleasure of doing her hair.*

More Visitors

Right, back again, do concentrate!

So much has happened in the years since you left. I am currently on my own, but still open to meeting new people, new encounters, still inviting people to have lunch with me and see my treasures at my ancient London house, which is now rather falling to pieces – the paintwork is appalling, especially in your room. But then I never use that.

One new person, female, who has recently come into my life is someone you did meet – Sophie, the daughter of Graham Watson. Do you remember him? Of course you do. He was the boss of Curtis Brown and your literary agent for most of your writing life, before he retired and then you had, oh God, what was she called? Australian woman – Tessa Sayle. She was a good, no-nonsense literary agent. But then she died.

One of the things about still working at my age is just how many agents and similar professional folks I have got through in my long-legged life. Professional people tend to retire at retiring age, if not before. But we freelances hang on till the bitter end. Two of my agents died too young, in their middle years — Richard Simon and Giles Gordon. I have had three accountants – two of them now retired. Three lawyers, two retired. As for editors, since I first joined *The Sunday Times* in 1960, there have been – let me see – eight editors: Harry Hodson, Denis Hamilton, Harry Evans, Frank Giles, Andrew Neil, John Witherow, Martin Ivens, Emma Tucker and now

Ben somebody. I've not met him. At the *New Statesman*, I have worked under five different editors since 1999. They all have gone – and I am still here, clinging on by my fingertips.

Graham Watson was a great literary agent, a gentleman of the old school, and he loved you dearly. You got yourself an agent in 1963, about a year before I did, as you had finished your first book before me. When I came to do a book, I contacted the same agency – but Graham did not want to look after me as well as you. So I got a new, younger agent in the firm called Richard Simon. He turned out to be the ideal agent for me and became a family friend, joining us on holidays. The children were amused that his nickname in his family was Teapot, so we always called him that.

Graham must have been about thirty years older than us but he and his wife, Dorothy, were ever so friendly. I can remember going to their new house in Primrose Hill beside the canal – and also visiting them in Lakeland, where they had a lovely farmhouse. We later visited them at Rye, where they rented the house where Henry James had lived. Graham died in 2002, aged eighty-nine, and we both went to his memorial service. He had two daughters, Sophie and Julia. We met them both when they were young, just teenagers, when we visited them in Lakeland. We later met Julia in Moscow, when we were invited by the Union of Russian Writers. She was married to Martin Walker, who was then the *Guardian*'s man in Moscow.

Anyway, after that long preamble down memory lane – hope you enjoyed the trek – Sophie Watson has moved into our area and has become a dear friend. She is a professor at the Open University and is a world expert on, come on... what do you think? Water. She has been living just two streets away, which I had not realised till a mutual friend, also a professor, and his wife, who live round the corner, mentioned that Sophie Watson knew me – so I invited them all to drinks in the garden and to see my treasures. Lucky them. Sophie then invited me back to her house, where I met her adopted daughter, Jessica, who is originally Chinese, and Sophie's partner, Russell. He is one of the regular early-morning swimmers at the Lido, all the year round.

Sophie has her own cosy, attractive study in their back garden – a large shed, but nicely decorated, heating and a bed.

I find her very entertaining and witty – well, for an academic. She took her first degree at Sussex, where Caitlin went, but has acquired plenty of other degrees since. She is professor of sociology and head of faculty at the Open University. She seems to know an awful lot about water. I have no idea how she got into it, but she certainly writes and lectures about it a great deal.

After a few drinks, I suggested we did a book together. On water. About which I know nothing. She would write the serious bits and I would write the fun ones, assemble some daft facts. I do this all the time. I meet someone who is an expert on something, become fascinated by what they do, and then get them excited about the idea of collaborating with me on a book. They think because I have had so many books published, it'll be easy for me to find a publisher for this one. Alas, no. I might have had a hundred books published – but I've also had a hundred books turned down. My latest fantastic idea to fall on deaf ears is 'Sex in Old Age'. Don't groan, or make a face, which is what Caitlin and Flora did. In fact, everyone made a face. Only two people thought it was a brilliant idea. Caitlin Moran of *The Times* has promised to give me a quote. Prue Leith, whom I met at an *Oldie* party, said, 'Oh, you can interview me for the book.' Alas, all the publishers I approached have turned it down. They are dominated these days by either thirty-something woke young women or suits from management central casting.

You will remember me being very disappointed when I failed to get a biography of Canon Rawnsley, the co-founder of the National Trust, off the ground. I got access to his letters, read all his books, but could not get a publisher interested. More recently, I thought I had a brilliant idea for a book narrating two parallel histories – the Football Association and the London Underground railway, both of which came into being in London in the same year, 1863. I collected some excellent material on the Underground, including original artwork by Harry Beck. But all my publishers said no: do one or the other – not both together.

Will I ever get to write a book about water with Sophie? I doubt it somehow. I have not said that to Sophie, needless to say. But I am hoping she will become one of my friends. Strictly platonic, of course. But we do have lots of laughs and enjoy the same sort of gossip.

MAX EGREMONT

I have another good friend who has been to lunch recently – Lord Egremont, also known as Max Egremont, a well-known writer and author of fourteen books. You and I both knew his mother – Pamela, Lady Egremont. You must remember her. She was a stunner, so elegant and well dressed, even in her late eighties. She lived most of the summer months at Cockermouth Castle and, during the thirty years we lived at Loweswater, she used to invite us for supper at the castle. We got to know her because she was a dear friend and fishing companion of our next-door neighbour Geoffrey White, formerly vicar of Loweswater. One year when we went for supper with her at the castle, I asked what she had been doing recently. She said, 'Oh, I just spent the last few months in Vietnam.' You what? She always looked like a fashion plate, so Vietnam did not seem a very glamorous place for a holiday. 'Doing what?' I asked. 'I was in a hospital,' she said. 'Oh, did you fall ill?' 'No, working. I was working as a nurse.' She had indeed trained as a nurse during the last war, and also worked on secret stuff at Bletchley Park. Before the war she was known as a great beauty, one of three Irish sisters who often appeared in the society mags.

I met Max, her elder son, about twenty years ago when we were both being published by the same publisher, Christopher Sinclair-Stevenson. Then, a few years ago, I happened to write about Lady Egremont in my *Cumbria Life* column and Max and I got in touch again. We had arranged lunch here at the house, but then the entire country was locked down because of the wretched pandemic, and we had to cancel. Anyway, he has just been here. I gave him a tour of my house and treasures – bit of a cheek on my part, really, when you think he has not just a castle in the north but an enormous stately home in the south. I took him for lunch at Bistro Laz. Over lunch we had some good fun, comparing Lakeland memories, stories about Pamela and our publishing experiences.

Years ago, I also met his dad – John Wyndham, the 1st Baron Egremont, who at one time was private secretary to Harold Macmillan when he was prime minister. I interviewed him for the Atticus column. So I had met both of Max's parents. It was strange talking about them, now long dead, when both Max and I are also getting on. Although Max is nobbut a lad, really, he's only seventy-four. I do like it when I can reminisce with people about their parents. It is a sign of my age, of course, but it's something I won't be able to do so much in the future, as the years pass. I don't think there is anybody alive who remembers my parents, except my sister Annabel and brother Johnny. My father, after all, died in 1957. As you get

older, it is rare to meet people whose parents you also knew...
When I meet Paul McCartney, who has now turned eighty, I
am able to reminisce about his dad, Jim, who I am sure very
few of Paul's other London friends can remember.

Max Egremont's main home is Petworth House in Sussex,
where, by chance, I did a talk in autumn 2022 at the Petworth
Literary Festival. I was picked up at Haslemere station and the
driver pointed out the walls of the Petworth estate, stretching
for about five miles. Over lunch at Bistro Laz, Max said that
the house had been given over to the National Trust in 1947
in lieu of death duties, but that he and his wife and family still
live in one-third of it and the family still own the estate.

We discussed books and he said he was working on a novel
at the moment, when he had time from his estate duties.
He had not yet found a publisher for it and he seemed a bit
pessimistic about getting a commission. We compared notes
and I went on about stupid publishers, how they can't spot
a really, really good idea when it is presented to them. He
did not quite concur, being such a traditional gentleman, so
polite and charming, never boasting or showing off or name-
dropping or mentioning his estates. This despite his owning
thousands of acres, including Petworth itself and large estates
in west Cumbria. When we owned our house and 14 acres
at Loweswater, I once noticed in our deeds that the mineral
rights on our fields did not belong to us but to the Leconfield
Estates. Which means his family. He is in fact the 7th Baron
Leconfield as well as the 2nd Baron Egremont.

At the end of our lunch, he invited me to come to Petworth
in the spring when he is in residence and have lunch and
a tour of the house and estate. 'I will hire a cook,' he said
as I put him on the bus. From the bistro, he was heading
for Lincoln's Inn to see the family lawyers. I thought about
that remark when I got home. Wished I had asked him

about hiring a cook. Do he and his wife, who is a landscape gardener, not cook? Do they live on takeaways? Or do they go out to eat all the time? Or has their cook done a runner? How the aristocracy live, eh? Just like the rest of us, is the answer. Only with more space.

I once went to interview Deborah, Duchess of Devonshire, one of the famous Mitford sisters, at Chatsworth. She talked non-stop about one of her passions in life – Elvis Presley. She had just visited Graceland. She also adored the Beatles and showed me a 1964 edition of *The Beatles Book Monthly*. After our chat, I needed to go to the lavatory, but I got lost and found myself in a big reception room with a curtained-off bit in the corner. I pulled the curtain aside – and there was the duke, sitting on his own, tucking into a plate of baked beans on toast. Yum yum.

Another time, when I was at Buckingham Palace, about to interview Prince Philip for BBC's *Bookshelf*, I was waiting in an anteroom with the producer, ready to be called into the presence. I was examining the bookshelves, looking for my own books, or yours, and by mistake I pressed a hidden button. The bookshelves swung open to reveal a secret door into a small sitting room – in which Prince Philip was seated on his own. He was crouching in front of an old-fashioned electric fire, with just one bar on. He jumped in surprise when I suddenly appeared, so I hastily retreated and waited for a uniformed flunkey to come and officially present us.

ROB AND ALI

Two other new friends you won't know are Rob and Alison. I met them about five years ago in Bequia. They were at the Bequia Beach Hotel where I was staying, on my own. Rob looked ever so trendy, aged about fifty-five, with long grey

1970s hair and loads of beads and bangles, jewellery and rings. I guessed he must have been in the pop world, perhaps a manager, or a roadie, even a member of a boy band, many years ago.

One evening at the bar, he came across and said that he loved my book. He had just heard my name and realised I had written one of his favourite books. I expected him to say *The Beatles* – but it was *The Glory Game*, my behind-the-scenes book about Tottenham Hotspur in the early 1970s. It was his bible when he was growing up.

I later had a meal with them – and at last found out what his job was. I would never have guessed it. He was an audiologist. You know – someone who provides hearing aids. You moaned in your last few years about me going deaf and refusing to do anything about it. Just as Caitlin and Flora do today. Could he be my saviour? He turned out to be more than just an ordinary high-street audiologist – I don't think many of them can afford the Bequia Beach Hotel. He is a celebrity audiologist. You what? Yes, I never realised they existed, but I should have done. You get celebrity hairdressers, dentists, doctors who attend to the rich and famous, so there must be celebrity audiologists. Except you don't read about them – for the simple reason that celebrities don't like to admit they are wearing hearing aids. Celebs today will happily go on in interviews about their cancer treatment, drug habits, alcohol abuse, depression, or being sexually abused as a child, but they never go on about their hearing problems. But hearing loss happens to everyone in time, especially to rock musicians. All those drums, my dears, the loud and throbbing electronic music, hammering your ears all your working life. No wonder their ears suffer.

Rob used to have premises in Harley Street and treated lots of well-known people. Now he has his clinic, Hearing

Healthcare Practice, in Harpenden, in Hertfordshire. The only name I managed to get out of him is of someone now dead – Michael Jackson. But he also mentioned in passing members of the Spanish royal family. His wife, Ali, works with him and they have a very successful practice. They found they did not need to be based in central London. Clients are prepared to come to them. I am going to get tested by him soon, when I get round to it, and get fitted for a decent pair of hearing aids. Damn the expense.

During that holiday when I first met him, going for swims and walks and meals together, can you guess what I did? I suggested to him we should do a book together – 'Hear Hear', all about the history of hearing, how and when it goes, and what you can do about it. I wrote out a proper proposal, featuring interviews with Rob, drawing on all his knowledge and experience. But can you believe it? It went the same way as 'Sex in Old Age' – turned down by everyone. However, Rob and I have remained friends. And last week he and Ali came for lunch. As with Max Egremont, we had booked a date during lockdown but had to cancel.

He is still going to help me with my hearing, give me some advice, despite our book idea not getting anywhere. So far. You have to live in hope. As long as you are living...

IAN JACK

Ian Jack was another who was due to come for lunch, as he did once or twice every year. But this time he never did. He has just died suddenly while at his holiday home on the Isle of Bute, aged only seventy-seven.

Since you died, I have got used to many of my contemporaries falling off their perch. Well, what do you expect, at our ages, so I tell myself. I am contacted all the time whenever someone

I worked with on *The Sunday Times* dies. It's on a sort of round-robin email thing, going to forty people. You are expected to reply or do a Zoom call and give your memories. I usually groan when I see it coming up and rarely respond. I am invited to a lot of funerals and memorials – but I never go. I almost always can remember the person who has died, and liked them, but, dear God, my friendship with them was decades ago, back in the sixties. I haven't seen them since. My life has moved on.

But with Ian Jack, I did feel a pang, a sadness, a bereavement. I have always kept in regular contact with him and loved him dearly. He never looked particularly robust or healthy – untidy and unfit-looking – but I never heard him complain about his health. Unlike me. He always seemed calm and quiet, wise and sensible, while I tend to be noisy and pushy, impulsive and overexcited. I did not know his actual age till I saw it in the obituaries. I suppose I had never asked him. I had assumed he was roughly my age, perhaps a year or two younger. I knew him for more than fifty years, back to 1970 when he first joined *The Sunday Times*. He was deputy chief sub but for some reason he used to help out on the Look pages, which I was editing, for Harry Evans, to get them started. I only did the job for six months, then went back to books. Ian later edited the section.

We became close friends, having Scotland in common. He still had a Scottish accent, whereas I lost mine years ago. We used to reminisce about Cambuslang, just outside Glasgow. One of Ian's first jobs was on the *Cambuslang Advertiser*, a paper long gone. Cambuslang was where my father's parents lived, and I had many holidays there when I was young. We were also both interested in steam trains and steamships, and would give each other old timetables and prints.

Ian was seriously well-read and a seriously good writer. His writing was a bit like him – not flash or showy, not shouting and showing off, the way most columnists do. He quietly got on with his story, drew you into his knowledge and thoughts and reflections, so you had to read on. You always learned something. It seemed so smooth and effortless, but he was in fact one of the slowest writers I ever knew. He took an age over every sentence, aiming for perfection. Not like me, dashing them off. As for books, he was commissioned to write several, but didn't manage to finish them all. At the time of his death, he was working on a book about the Clyde. I remember many years ago an early feature he did in *The Sunday Times* about two estate agents. A boring subject on the face of it, but London prices were rocketing and all sorts of flash-Harry estate agents were appearing on the scene. Ian's piece was so revealing and entertaining. Nothing he said about them was unfair or nasty, so they could not sue, but he caught them exactly – their cockiness, their tricks of the trade, their smug patter – revealing a new urban species whose emergence none of the rest of us had really noticed.

Ian's obituaries in all the papers were extensive and laudatory, especially in the *Guardian*, where he had done a Saturday column for the last fifteen years, and in *The Times*. He also edited the *Independent on Sunday* and *Granta*. The outpouring of love and affection for him from so many people, both writers and readers, was remarkable. I had somehow thought I was the only person who realised how kind and wise and talented he was.

As a broadsheet journalist, he was most unusual. Partly because he was a non-graduate, leaving school to work as a librarian and then on local papers. But he never mentioned that. He never went on about his background, or overcompensated, or showed off his knowledge. Nor did he appear regretful or jealous of those who had gone to Oxbridge. He was so humble and gentle, most unusual for a journalist. He never told you what a great column he had just written, which most of us do, or was desperate for praise or recognition. 'Have you read my piece...?' is a common greeting among journalists. He was so quiet and modest and unpushy that a stranger might wonder how he had come to rise so high up the editorial ladder in so many different publications. I think it was because, when you got to know him and his work, you were aware of his wisdom, maturity and good sense. You trusted his opinion.

He never tried to hold the floor or dominate the conversation, take over the dinner table. He came often to our house, and you liked him as well. He did not say much, just sat there, amused, listening. You invited him to my fortieth birthday do in 1976, a surprise dinner party you organised behind my back, inviting people you knew were my best and oldest friends, without telling me. You ordered very high-quality Châteauneuf-du-Pape. You got it through the Hallgartens, who lived opposite and whose family was in the wine business. Remember?

Ian came – and, to my surprise, brought a girlfriend I had never seen before. A very interesting woman in the theatre. We never saw her again. For someone so unmacho, unsmooth, unhandsome, Ian always seemed to have an attractive, bright girlfriend. He married a beautiful Indian woman during a period of his life when he was passionate about India. That marriage did not last. Then he married Lindy and went on to have two children. She had been a sub on the *Indy*. She went to Somerville, your old college, and was lovely and clever. They came to visit us in the Lake District. It was the first time we had met Lindy. She was rather trendy and modern – compared with Ian, with his straggly beard and generally tramp-like appearance.

Ian sacked me once. It was when he was editor of the

SIndy. I was doing a weekly column, which was his idea, then after about six months, it did not appear one Sunday morning. Oh well, I thought, they had no space, busy week, lots of adverts, I know what happens in papers, it will be in next week. About ten o'clock there was a knock at the front door and Ian was there, looking rather nervous. I invited him in for coffee and croissants. It took him a while to explain his unexpected early-morning visit. Eventually, he said he was sacking me – and had come to do so in person. I laughed aloud at his discomfort. In my long life as a jobbing columnist, with usually several columns on the go at any one time, I have been sacked several times. I never take offence. After all, the person doing the sacking usually gets sacked themselves, in the end. You have to take it in your stride.

It was so kind and gracious of Ian to take the time to traipse across from Islington on a Sunday morning to break it to me in person. His explanation for my sacking, when it eventually emerged, was bollocks. Well, that was what I chose to think. It was mainly, he said, to do with the women in the office, who were getting upset that the paper had so many male columnists. One of them had to go. And that person happened to be me. I told him I did not take it personally. And we remained friends for the rest of his life.

For decades, Ian was one of the five male friends with whom I lunched once a year, just the two of us, to talk about our families, wives, children, houses, money, ailments, triumphs, disappointments. I still have an annual lunch with Melvyn Bragg, probably my oldest friend in London. We came from Cumbria about the same time, back in 1960. I also see Ray Connolly, another journalist, once a year. He had Covid so badly he was in a coma for months.

Michael Bateman was another old journalist friend I had known since my Durham days – he was at Oxford, but his first job was on the *Durham Advertiser* and he covered university affairs. Alas, he died a few years ago.

I also still have my German friend, Otmar. He lives in Bequia in the West Indies, so it's hard to drop in on him, but I hope to visit him this coming January, if I can find someone to go with. I have known Otmar for thirty years, since you and I first stayed with him at the Old Fort. I have lunch with him when I am there, and we compare notes on our love lives, if there is anything to compare...

Ian Jack came to your funeral service in 2016 at Golders Green. He arrived late as he was working that day but came back to the house for the drinks. You would have been pleased to see him. I do miss him. Though I am sure not as much as his wife Lindy and their two children do. Ian was loved and admired by so many. I hope I will be half as lucky when my time comes...

Rest in peace, which I am sure you are doing, all the time.

LETTER THIRTEEN

*Wardington Cycle Club, 1980s. We bought a
holiday cottage in this pretty Oxfordshire village.
How we fancied ourselves on our bikes. Such fun.*

More Ops

Hi, pet, how are you fizzing, how is your mother off for dripping?

That is a wartime greeting – very popular when I was at primary school in Dumfries. Doesn't make much sense now – or then, really.

Anyway, how are you? Escaped Covid?

Sorry, I forgot you are now immortal. No need to worry about your health anymore. Just lie back on your cloud all day and think lovely thoughts. Meanwhile, you have asked how I am getting on down here... Okay, you didn't, but I am sure from time to time you have been wondering how the old feller is.

I told you earlier about my triple heart bypass, lucky you, which is now so long ago I can't remember it. All the scars have long gone, but I am still taking five pills a day, which I will have to forever, until I join you on your cloud. So boring. I am always forgetting. I am convinced the blood thinner, which is only soluble aspirin, is making my arms turn black and blue with the slightest knock. If I have a teeny scratch, which I am not aware of, it bleeds and bleeds. Just a surface scratch, not even a wound. I often wake up in the night with the sheets covered with blood, and realise I must have scratched my leg while gardening.

After the bypass, I had another op – this time for a hernia. Some branch of the Royal Free, miles away in north London.

I have wiped it from my mind, so I will spare you the details, yet it loomed large at the time.

Isn't the mind clever, the way it can forget unpleasant things? Once you had your double mastectomy – back in 1972, or was it 1974? – I honestly did forget about it. For about forty years. Until your cancer came back.

I had a bit of a funny turn on the Isle of Wight last summer. I was invited by my neighbours to join them in their new hot tub. I was hoping it might be an orgy. But all we did was drink. When I eventually staggered home, the husband, Neil, opened my front door and checked I had got in. I managed to struggle up the stairs. Then I fell down, twice, all the way. There was blood everywhere. My arms and legs were black and blue. I had head wounds and chest pains. What a mess. In the night, I started coughing up blood.

I don't know how I got back to London next day. Living on my own is worrying enough when I am fully fit. I have to manage so many forms of transport that I always fear I will miss connections and, if I fall, no one will know where I am. Anyway, I made it home to London and decided I had better go straight to the Royal Free, to have everything checked. I have not registered with a GP on the Isle of Wight yet, nor even worked out where the local hospital is. And, as you know, I have not got a car. I am lucky in London that I can walk to my GP and also to the Royal Free, just across the Heath.

I spent six hours in A&E. Oh gawd. All forms of life are there, an endless pageant of the sick and wounded, all types and ages and nationalities, continually passing in front of you. It seemed like a back projection, a montage, a hologram of the human condition. I nearly left at the beginning, as at the top of the first queue was a tramp with six carrier bags, a well-spoken, bearded tramp… well, this is Hampstead. He was dirty and scruffy, but probably much younger than me. He was swearing at the receptionist because she wanted him to put on a mask. He said it was his citizen's right not to. He said Charing Cross had not asked him to wear one, or the Chelsea and Westminster, or any other hospital. He then went through all his hospital appointments. His stories were incoherent but graphic and well described. I was listening at first, quite amused, but very soon I was screaming inside, wanting him to hurry up, telling myself just five more minutes, and then I am out of here.

The receptionist had clearly got fed up with him as well. Six security men suddenly arrived to confront him. They held him by the arms, took him to one side. They managed to calm him down and persuade him to put on a mask. The queue began to move at last, thank God. And I got to see a doctor. But for the next two hours, I kept finding myself in the same queues as the posh tramp. He was waiting in the same corridors for the same nurses, same doctors, same scans. I had to listen to him telling his same hospital stories. In the end, though, I had all the tests I needed. It turned out I hadn't broken anything. The reason I had coughed up blood was that I had bashed into a banister and slightly damaged the lining of my lung. But that particular problem should now have stopped and I just had to keep an eye on it.

Are you still there? Or have you gone to sleep? I don't blame you. Hospital stories are almost as boring as travel stories.

Oh, I am sorry, there is another medical saga I must share. A couple of months ago I had an operation in a private hospital. Yes, I went private. Don't scream. I have not let the side down. The private operation I had was for a cataract. And it was free. My high-street optician in Kentish Town has for several years been telling me I have cataracts in both eyes, normal for my age, but they will get worse and need to be corrected. He said the waiting list on the NHS is one year. I said I hope I live that long. But then he added that there was a new scheme whereby he could refer patients to a private hospital – where it would be done for free. I would only have to wait around six weeks. I immediately agreed.

Cataract surgery is the commonest operation in the UK – some 400,000 of us have it every year. Everyone gets older and everyone's eyesight fades. In the UK, we are all living longer, so NHS queues are getting longer all the time.

I was eventually called to the Optegra Eye Hospital in Colindale, north London. It was in a new building, on a small industrial estate, well-appointed if not quite luxurious. There was no free coffee, tut tut, as the machine was on the blink – but lots of attentive staff. First hour was endless tests, forms filled, loads of eye drops, before I entered the operating theatre, where about four bustling gowned-up nursing staff got me ready. The surgeon, Dr Moayedi, who turned out also to be the medical director, was a mature, sensible-looking man in his fifties. I trusted him at once. Using ultrasound, it took him just fifteen minutes to remove the cloudy lens behind my pupil and replace it with a plastic lens. Amazing. I asked him afterwards how many he did in a day. 'Thirty,' he replied. 'I could do forty, but my staff are so slow.' This was clearly meant as a wind-up. Office banter. Sorry, *operating theatre* banter. There was some eye-rolling on the part of the staff in question. 'I must have done 40,000 cataract operations in my career so far,' Dr Moayedi concluded. No wonder it is Britain's number one op. And from start to finish, it was all done in two hours.

So how much did I save? Just been online and I see that in Harley Street and elsewhere you can pay £2,500 per eye. So I saved myself £5,000 – counting the other eye when it gets done. And they gave me a free plastic eye shield, which I had to wear at night. What a bargain, eh? And I also have the warm glow of having helped the NHS to reduce its waiting lists.

My dear Margaret, I hope you have read all this without yawning or skipping. I have stuck to your principle of seeking medical advice when ailments continue, so well done me. Being ill and poorly in old age is just so boring and so time-consuming. When you were here, I would ignore your advice that I should stop moaning and go and see a doctor at once. Now I'm on my own I feel I have to be sensible, get things checked and have the tests my GP says I need.

I had some more tests the other week when a young GP did a full examination. He finished by putting his gloved hand up my bum and announced I had an enlarged prostate. In fact, it was so large he feared it might be cancerous. Thanks a lot. Glad I dropped by… In the last few years, I have started getting up for a wee as much as four or five times a night, which is apparently a sign of prostate problems. But I have always got up in the night, so it did not worry me. It's hardly surprising, given the amount of wine I drink – a bottle a day, though of course I lie if the doctor asks. I had to have blood tests, which were inconclusive. So that was good news, I suppose. But then the doctor insisted on some different tests. For a couple of weeks, I was in and out of the surgery all the time. At least it was the practice nurse who was doing the tests, and I didn't have to drag myself over to the Royal Free. The upshot was that my prostate is enlarged but is not cancerous, so far. I was told there are two types of medication I could take to reduce the size of my prostate, each of which can have side-effects. I said thanks, but no thanks. I will live with having to get up to pee in the night for the moment. And await events.

So that is it, really, my medical highlights of the last six years or so. You are now up to date.

Enjoy. I am only telling you because you are my age. Well, two years younger. I have this rule never to go on about my health with any of the younger generation. They don't want to hear. They can see you are old, so what do you expect, at your age? If anyone asks me how I am, I always say fine thanks, still here.

The tally of operations I've had is fairly modest, I think, for someone in their late eighties. I have recovered from all the dramas and alarms so far. I consider myself pretty fit for my age: I walk about four miles a day and swim three times a week. My walking, though, is getting worse, I'm staggering all over the place; my limbs creak and crack and groan. But really, I can cope. I feel I can still look after myself on my own and do most things I want to do, whenever I get the chance to do those things I really, really want to do. No need to spell them out. You will just be appalled, like Caitlin and Flora are.

I know I go on about being a bit deaf or about my back aching or staggering, and about how I hope one day soon to find another girlfriend, but, dear God, I should not be moaning or complaining. I am so lucky to be here, at the age of eighty-six, fairly fit, and still working and rushing around.

Have you heard about poor Johnny? Compared with him, my life is a doddle. I mean Johnny my brother, who, as you know, is five years younger than me, taller, handsomer, fair-haired, fitter. You were most taken with him when you first came into our family life some sixty-five years ago. Johnny was then a young apprentice electrician, and he later moved into social work. He retired about fifteen years ago. Still lives in Carlisle with his wife, Marjory.

You will be horrified to hear he has just had both his feet amputated. I know, I could not believe it either. In this day and age, with all our so-called miracle operations, wonder treatments and transplants. He appears to have had circulation problems exacerbated by diabetes. The result was that both his feet turned black and blue, giving him constant pain, night and day. He had endless tests and medications, but in the end they decided amputation was the only way to stop the pain in his feet. It sounds medieval, like something from the Dark Ages. I rang him yesterday to see how he was. He sounded remarkably stoical, even cheerful, saying he is so pleased the pain is over. The best thing is he can now have uninterrupted sleep.

For Christmas, I am going to buy him an electric wheelchair. One of those nifty modern ones, sleek and red, like a racing car, so he can whizz into Carlisle whenever he wants a pint.

At least he is still alive. Unlike you...

LETTER FOURTEEN

*Christmas card, 1972. The Davieses dressed as an
Edwardian family. Flora had just been born. A posed
picture taken by our friend Frank Herrmann.*

Online Dates

Shield your eyes, pet.

I've been on my first blind date. The first date since I split with the girlfriend I had well over a year ago now. Yes, I know, pathetic and sad at my age, Caitlin and Flora both think. But a year on my own, without a special female friend in my life, just to talk to, walk with, tell things to, has been pretty dreary. I have loads to do, loads of chums, including female ones, as I have told you, but they are either married or have made it clear they just want to be platonic friends. In my fantasy, I want to find someone in the next few months, sympathetic, amusing, interested, affectionate, compatible, who I can invite to the West Indies in January. I am desperate to get away, while I still have the energy, even if I have to go on my own. Several female friends have said yes, lovely, I'll come, you can treat me, but of course separate bedrooms.

I had high hopes of an attractive lawyer, someone I had met years ago, who wrote to me, suggesting a drink, and then came for a meal. She seemed very keen. She mentioned she had been married, which was hardly unexpected for an attractive woman of her age, around sixty-five. Then it came out she'd been married to a woman. Who she still shares a house with, though they now go their separate ways. I was rather taken aback. Nothing wrong with women marrying women, or women living with women, of course – my sister Marion did that for many years, very happily. But since the woman had made the first approach, her lesbian history took me by surprise. She did not appear to be the person I was looking for.

So what am I looking for? To find out, I decided to go back on Saga dating. You may remember that I did that three years ago and found it fascinating and productive. One of the attractions this time was that it was going to be free. I do a column in *Saga* magazine – have done for two years. I love doing it – it's actually my best-paid column, pro rata. I write about personal things, trying to be amusing – you know, the sort of stuff I have done for ages. It is mainly about Love in Old Age, but recently I have been struggling to find things to write about it, since I have not had a regular girlfriend for quite a while. One of my *Saga* editors suggested they could arrange for me to have three months free on Saga's dating site. You know how I am a sucker for anything free.

Unlike you. You hated anything free. You would refuse things in shops, on the street, if someone came up and offered you something free. Whereas I would always grab it. Any special offers, deals, three for the price of two, have me slavering. When you became seriously ill and I had to do the shopping, you always wrote NO BARGAINS at the top of the list. I still have copies, in your immaculate high-school handwriting.

I revealed my true age and used a photo only one week old. But I somehow mucked up my list of requirements about what sort of woman I was after. By mistake, I ticked a box that stated I was looking for a wealthy woman. Silly me. At my age, I do find it very confusing, filling in forms online. Perhaps I need a PA, not just a partner. After a lot of faffing around, I finally managed to set up my Saga profile, and the offers came flooding in. Oh yes.

The first woman I met had not included her photo in her

profile, which was a bit worrying. Did that mean she was famous, or that she was married and did not want her husband to know? Or was she so stunning she would be besieged with offers? Nor did I know her real name. She answered to the name 'Petal', which I also found a bit worrying. I didn't know her age either, but assumed she must be between sixty-five and seventy-five, which is the age range I said I was interested in.

In fact, I am not sure why I agreed to meet her, when I knew so little about her. But she had sounded nice and friendly and bright in her messages and in our phone calls. She had been some sort of businesswoman. At my age, you can't muck around, or spend too much time in idle chat-ups. And she suggested meeting for a coffee in Hampstead, which was ideal, as it saved me having to trek into town or out into the suburbs.

Last time I went on Saga dating, I'd met a nice woman who lived miles out in the wilds of Hertfordshire. It took me ages getting there from Marylebone station when she invited me to her house for lunch. It is partly snobbish, not wanting a lady friend who lives too far from NW5, NW3 or N6. But it's also my age. I can't be doing with long journeys out of my comfort zones anymore. Then she moved to Cornwall, so that settled it. I never contacted her again. Oh, it is a cruel business, online dating. You have to make instant suppositions, agreements, decisions.

I told the woman who called herself Petal that I would be wearing a red scarf. Petal said she would be wearing a pink sweater. I hoped the café wasn't full of women of a certain age wearing pink sweaters. Could have been embarrassing if I went up to the wrong one.

But Petal came over to me the minute I entered the café. She had of course seen my phizog in my profile photo, and had spotted my red scarf. She led me to a small table with two seats, the only ones vacant. It was a Saturday morning in Hampstead and the coffee bars are always busy. She started fussing that the table was too small and the seats uncomfortable. She preferred her usual table, but someone had bagged it. She glared around, trying to see if anyone was about to leave. She then spotted a man at a table on his own. She went over and asked him to swap with us, saying he was sitting at her favourite table, awfully sorry, did he mind moving? Oh my God, what a palaver. She was charming enough, smiling at the poor man, but did this mean she was a fusspot, a Bossy Betty, always wanting to get her own way? Or was she really a kind, caring person, thinking only of my comfort?

We ordered our coffees and eventually she settled herself. After some idle chat about how busy the caff was, and how often she came here, I asked her some personal questions. One of the many good things about online dating is that you know people are looking for some sort of relationship. Otherwise, why would they be meeting you? But what kind of relationship? Ahh, *that* is what has to be slowly discovered.

I asked her how long she had been online dating – and she was immediately off, telling me about all the awful men she had met over the years. 'They tend to want one of three things: sex, someone to look after them, or they are looking to move in.' She had apparently recently met a sequence of men – well-spoken, educated – who had gone through expensive divorces and were currently living in rented accommodation. They had clearly worked out from her profile and brief chats that she had her own house in Hampstead, which is what she had told me in our warm-up phone calls. When they found that out, she said, their main object was to move in with her. And of course not pay any rent. I could not believe she would ever fall for that. She appeared too smart. She had been married, to a professor of medicine, but he was a geek, interested only in his work, and not in her. He never sympathised when she had had a hard day at her work. He just thought about his own day. She was talkative enough, telling me about her life and work, but I began to have a headache, listening to her chuntering on. We clearly had nothing in common. I was not interested in her interests, such as playing bridge and going to classical concerts. She did not listen to Radio 4 or read any of the newspapers and magazines I read. She was neat and attractive enough, with dyed blonde hair, but I did not fancy her. There was clearly no chemistry between us.

After forty minutes, I paid for the coffees and said I had to go home as I had some work to do. She did not look too disappointed. Oh well. It was a start, of a sort, getting back into the dating groove again. Can't give up now, can I, after just one failure?

But online dating does take up a lot of time. It can become a full-time occupation. You have to keep an eye on the dating site all the time, looking out for new clicks, matches, messages, and then send suitably appealing comments back, with enticing details and amusing comments, if somebody appears to be vaguely interested. When you are sent matches telling you Pretty Polly or Sexy Sue is interested in you, and would like to hear from you, you can then send them a one-line personal message. It does not go direct to them at this stage, but via the site. So they still don't know who or where you are. If they then reply to you, at this stage you can give them your real email address and phone number, so they can ring and chat. If that goes well, you can arrange to meet, for a coffee or whatever.

I was contacted by several women who appeared to have been online for ages – though they rarely admitted exactly how long. But it soon emerges and you suspect that online dating is their hobby, their daily routine – even their full-time occupation. Yet they never seem to get anywhere, otherwise why are they still online? I asked one or two of them on the phone why they had apparently had little luck so far, and they said, oh, they were too choosy, too picky. That is another good thing about online dating – it gives you licence to put cheeky, personal questions to people you do not yet know. Not that it has ever stopped me asking cheeky, personal questions in normal life… You were always telling me off for asking people intimate things. And I always replied: they don't have to answer, I am just showing interest in them. With online dating, that is the whole point of the first meeting, in the flesh – to find out things about the other person. Okay, it is not the very first thing. The very, very first thing, for both parties, is to decide if you like them or fancy them. Is there any chemistry between you and them? This can happen quickly and at any age, oh yes it can, don't argue. That desire to get to know someone better, to be with them, never goes. And of course the opposite is also true. That can happen just as quickly as well. You can be repelled just as quickly as attracted.

What you hope is to feel a warmth. Physically speaking, I think it is important to like not just the look of the other person but their skin. And to want to touch it. I think that really is the clue to desire. If the skin attracts. While I am trying to work out whether I am really attracted to a person or not, I always want to find out as much about them as I can. I never think I have wasted my time if for an hour I have been able to look into another person's life, learn about their background, their family, where they have lived, what they have done, even before you get on to why their marriage collapsed, or how their husband died. I love all that. I feel enriched by learning about a total stranger. Even when I already know I am never going to see them again.

I then agreed to another date, with a likely-sounding

woman who suggested lunch in a brasserie in Camden. She was seventy-five, or so she had said, and seemed very fit, having walked right across Regent's Park and Primrose Hill to meet me. Or so she said. She was a retired solicitor and had gone to a very good university. I do like clever women. Always have done. She was divorced, and had two daughters. 'I have two daughters as well,' I said brightly. I went on: 'What do your daughters do? Are they married, do they live near you?' All harmless, routine questions, or so it seemed to me.

'Why are you asking me this?' she barked, glaring at me. 'You are supposed to be asking me about me.' 'But your children are you,' I replied. 'I will get a picture of you and your life by knowing something about them. I mean, do they live far away, perhaps in Australia? Now that can be tough. Or do they live near you in London? Even round the corner. That is always nice...'

I chuntered on about how one of my daughters had lived for fifteen years in Botswana... and what a drag it had been getting there. But now two of my children live locally and one on the south coast. So they are all quite close by, which is lovely. So tell me more about your own daughters? But again she glared at me, as if asking innocent questions about her daughters was out of bounds, private and personal. I usually find that imparting personal stuff about my own life and family encourages others to do the same. I often reveal really rather personal things before they have even asked me any questions. But this time it did not work. For some reason, her children were off limits. And she never told me why. So that was it. If she was not going to reveal totally harmless stuff about her family, I suspected I was never going to get to know her, far less want to touch her skin.

That's it, I decided. I think I will give up online dating forever. Takes too much time and is unlikely to lead anywhere.

Caitlin and Flora are right. It is pathetic, someone of my age looking for a girlfriend...

Pathetic... but fun. Sometimes.

LETTER FIFTEEN

On holiday at Windermere, 1980s. Windswept but awfully rugged.

Meeting Miranda

Who is she? Read on...

In the late summer of 2022, I decided to go to the Isle of Wight for four weeks, the longest time I have ever spent there, as I had so many events on. I was still wondering what to do about the house, now I was single again. I felt guilty every time I left it empty, as I do love it so much. In just two years I have acquired so many good friends and discovered so many lovely walks, places and people all over the island.

The book I had written about the island, finished a year earlier, was at last coming out, so I had several publishing events lined up. One was the launch party on the actual publication day to be held in Monkton Arts, right behind my house in Ryde, so very handy to get to. Another was a signing session at the Medina Bookshop in Cowes. That would be harder to get to as I don't drive and for some reason the local buses, brilliant though they are, do not go direct from Ryde to Cowes. You have to change at Newport. The third and most important event was the first-ever Isle of Wight Book Awards. I was deeply regretting starting this. In the first flush of enthusiasm for the island, I had decided to give something back and had mentioned the idea of a book festival to the owner of the Medina Bookshop, who had been most enthusiastic and said that they would support it. The island needed something like this – there was so much literary talent around.

It turned out to be a huge success, with over a hundred

entries, and I enlisted excellent judges in the form of Alan Titchmarsh and Joanna Trollope. The awards received the backing of some top-class island sponsors, who contributed towards the prizes and the costs of the grand awards lunch. I based the idea and the format on the Lakeland Book of the Year awards, which I set up thirty-eight years ago. It now has a life of its own, with lots of people involved, and I do very little except act as a judge. But having sold up in Loweswater after you died, it had become a fag going up each year for the awards lunch, especially now that I am on my own. So last year I resigned as a judge, but I will still continue to help fund it. You never realise how much work and expense is involved in such apparently simple events. I have arranged in my will that a donation I have given to the Cumbria Community Fund will fund it, till my money runs out. I donated the same amount of money as I did to Marie Curie: £50,000. I don't even think the children know what I did. They would be surprised. As would various friends, since I am always boasting about what a right tight bastard I am.

The book launch went off well, and my editor, Richard, kindly came all the way to the Isle of Wight to help. I ordered far too much wine, expecting many more people would come. But the roads were all blocked off around Ryde that evening, in preparation for the carnival. Several people who hadn't turned up told me later that they gave up trying to park and went home.

The Book Awards lunch was held at the Island Sailing Club in Cowes and was packed out; there was a large and excited audience and excellent speeches. We even got BBC TV South to come over from Southampton and film a feature for their evening show.

A rather posh woman in a large floppy hat came up to me at the Book Awards and said how much she had enjoyed it. Then she went into a long story about you – yes, you, Margaret Forster – about that book you did on Carr's of Carlisle. Your history of the biscuit factory, which you wrote decades ago. It turned out that she had been at school with one of the Carrs. She was a fan of all your books, she said. So that was nice. I love it when out of the blue someone starts talking about how they love your books. When I sat down again, someone whispered to me that the woman was Lady Grylls, a greatly loved character on the island, mother of the TV explorer and Chief Scout Bear Grylls. I had heard of him but never seen him, as I don't watch TV.

The book-signing session at the Cowes bookshop was more low-key – just a forty-minute chat to thirty or so locals. My friend Peter from Seaview kindly agreed to drive me there. I promised to buy him a meal afterwards. The bookshop was full when we got there, all seats taken. Paul, the shop manager, introduced me nicely but he had not provided a chair for me, expecting me to stand up to talk. Come on, Paul, I said. I can't stand up for forty minutes, don't you know how old I am? So he got me a chair, which meant I could at least see the front row. But I did not put on my specs, which I normally wear for long distance, so I could not see further than the front row. But it all seemed to go well; they laughed at my jokes, enjoyed hearing about the many things I love about their island.

The queue for buying books was quite long and it took ages to get through. I always try to have a few words with anyone kind enough to buy one of my books – which often leads to a longer chat than I really wanted, when by that time I am getting tired and am dying for a drink. Publishers love it when authors do signing sessions in bookshops – or anywhere, really – as long as it does not cost them much. I have done many a signing since my first book came out back in... oh, I can't remember, back in the 1960s.

One reason publishers love signing sessions is that they are always keen for their authors to be *seen*. Even if the bookshop doesn't end up selling that many books, they have to order quite a few and do a window display – which is great for local publicity. You gave up doing signings many years ago. You said you wanted to conserve your strength. Anyway, you had always believed that it is the publisher's job to push and sell a book, not the author's. I disagreed. Both have to do their bit. God knows, most books sell so few copies anyway that I don't know how publishers survive. And most authors.

The last person in the queue was a woman in her seventies who had been waiting patiently for some time. I noticed she had on a colourful scarf and a multicoloured knitted jacket and looked rather arty. Not a hippie. Just interesting and attractive. While I signed her book, I asked if she was local. She said yes, she lived here, near Cowes. She had come with a friend, who had got the two tickets for them. The friend had gone home straight after my talk. But she wanted to wait and buy my book. How kind, I said.

I found myself asking her what she was doing now and if she would like a drink. A bit pushy and presumptuous, I know. I added quickly that I was with my friend, Peter from Seaview, who had driven me here, and we were just about to go across the road to the Island Sailing Club for a glass of wine. Would she care to join us? She appeared a bit hesitant at first, trying to remember what it was she had planned for the evening. Having thought for a few moments and trying to remember where she had parked her car, she said okay then, a quick drink would be lovely.

The quick drink progressed into a couple. 'I like your pashmina, pet,' I said, in my light-hearted jocular northern way, showing off my fashion knowledge. 'It is a scarf, not a pashmina. And don't call me pet.' I liked that. Sign of character.

We moved on to us all having a pizza at the bar, plus salad, chatting all the while – well, to be strictly accurate, I was asking her questions non-stop. Her name was Miranda and she was an artist with a studio in Gurnard, which I had never heard of, but it is outside Cowes. Peter, meanwhile, was starting to roll his eyes. Miranda said the friend she had been with was blonde and very attractive. I would have liked her. I must have noticed her. I said I had honestly not noticed either of them during my talk. They must have been sitting at the back. She said she had teased her friend during my talk that, while I was talking, I was staring at her. Bollocks. I said... Excuse my language. I did not have my specs on. Truthfully, I could not see further than the front row.

By now, Peter was very amused by my chatting up Miranda. It was like being out with two teenagers, he said. And in truth, that is how I felt. Nothing really ever changes in male–female relationships, if the chemistry is there. People chat each other up and engage in mild flirting, however old and decrepit they might be. I learned that Miranda was originally from Norfolk, came from farming stock, and had at one time been at what is now Norwich University College of the Arts. She had been living on the island for forty years. She had been married but was divorced a long time ago and had two grown-up sons and three grandchildren. I also managed to find out, being ever so subtle, that she was not living with anyone, male or female, and did not appear to have a regular partner, female or male. But she clearly had lots of friends, lots of interests and activities. Apart from her own art work, she works in a hospice with dementia patients, where she is a practitioner of something called creative arts reminiscence. She described in detail a large collage she was making with elderly patients at the hospice, illustrating their life and memories, which would go on show soon in Cowes. It sounded interesting, though I did not quite understand how it worked. I like women who are active and have interests. And did she own her house? I forgot to ask that, but I think she implied she did.

I persuaded her to tell me her full professional name and said I would look it up on the internet, and find out more about her and what sort of art she does. If I can manage the internet, that is. She said she is the same, useless on the internet.

I have never been out with an artist before. I tend to be attracted to writers or media people, folks I can relate to professionally, so it would be interesting to get to know an artist. For some reason, on Saga dating I seem to have been attracted to professional women, like barristers and academics, none of whom I really have much in common with. Anyway, I had given all that up. Dating had been a waste of time. I was going to be content to be on my own from now on...

I told Miranda that my daughters, Caitlin and Flora, both went to art college, at least for an art foundation year, inheriting their artistic talents from their mother, not from me. I told her about my house in Ryde. Grade II listed, don't you know, minutes from the beach. Where I lived alone, not having a lady friend. Hint hint. Then I found myself inviting her to come and see it some time, have a drink, perhaps a walk on the beach? Peter's eye-rolling was becoming more intense.

I asked Miranda to write down her email address and said I would contact her, give her my address and suggest a date. She said thanks, I am sure your house must be lovely. She often came over to that side of the island for her art therapy work.

Well, that was an interesting evening, I said to Peter as he drove me home. A date without looking for it, a spark out of the dark, something I really did not expect when I set off with Peter to give a talk in a bookshop I had never been to before, in a town I did not know, in front of people I had never met. Where might it end, I wondered, as we drove back to Ryde.

They always say such things happen when you are not looking for it. Fate or what, eh? Not that I believe in fate. I believe you make your own luck. You have to work at it, make it happen. And I had, I suppose, by chatting her up all evening. We shall see...

When I got home there was an email from Lady Grylls, my new friend from the Book Awards lunch, signing herself Sally, and inviting me to come to her house to meet the Empress of Bembridge. On reading it properly, this turned out to be a pet pig she keeps in her back garden. She was inviting me as her guest to an event at the Bembridge Sailing Club. And if I liked, I could come to her place first, have a swim, and she would wear her bikini... Oh my goodness, what is happening now? Not just one but two well-bred, attractive ladies of a certain age wanting to be my friend...

What a hustler. Will he never change?

LETTER SIXTEEN

Margaret at a literary awards ceremony, 1989, with some fellow literary ladies: Penelope Lively, P. D. James, Hilary Mantel and Rose Tremain, plus Colin Thubron.

Discovering Miranda

Hi again. I bet you have been waiting, panting for the latest update on my affairs. I don't suppose you get much gossip up there...

I accepted Sally Grylls' invite and went to the event at Bembridge Sailing Club – lunch and a talk about the local wildlife on the Solent. The club is beautiful and I had long wanted to get inside, ever since I trespassed in the grounds during lockdown and managed to walk round it, sneaking a look at the architecture from the outside. The Royal Yacht Squadron at Cowes is grander and bigger, but I think the Bembridge is more attractive, homely and friendly. There are so many yacht clubs on the Isle of Wight. In my mind, before I came, I thought there would just be one. I still hear about ones I never knew existed.

But, alas, there was no swim with Sally beforehand. The day was cold and rainy. But she is a laugh, a character, our Sally, and I hope to keep seeing her when I am on the island. But we are just good friends. Especially now I have met Miranda. I am telling myself that Miranda could be my new Best Friend. Which is a bit presumptuous as I have only just met her.

But I invited Miranda to come to Ryde to see me at home. And she eventually agreed. Oh rapture.

I took her quickly round the house, showed her the West Wing, as I call it, a bedroom at the back down a corridor with an en suite bathroom. I made her some coffee and then I suggested a walk along the beach before dark, which is what I do all the time and love so much. We walked along Ryde Sands, talking all the way, to the Dell Café, my favourite caff. But curses, it was closed when we got there. Autumn had come and they were closing earlier than usual. I had left it too late. I was so disappointed. Mainly because I was knackered. My knee and back were playing up and I was desperate for a sit-down. But I did not moan much or reveal my aches and pains, not at this stage in a relationship. Don't want to appear my age, any more than is obvious. I managed to drag myself back, with lots of stops, pretending I just wanted to look at the sea and the ships and the sunset.

I gave Miranda a meal in my courtyard, smoked salmon and some quiche, quickly heated up in the microwave. Accompanied by Marlborough Sauvignon Blanc, my favourite. I know how to treat a gel. It began to grow chilly but she said she would still like to stay outside, as my courtyard was so attractive, which pleased me. I love eating outside, even in the autumn.

I went inside to get her my old overcoat. You know the one – the grey and black tweed one that I love, had it for years, one of the most expensive items I have ever bought. Or did you buy it for me? It is now rather moth-eaten, but I took it down to Ryde when I moved in, thinking it would be good for beach walks in the winter. And I left it here, as I now have a lighter winter overcoat, a black cashmere, rather stylish for me, to wear in London. As Miranda was putting on my overcoat, she noticed the label. 'Aquascutum! I used to work for them,' she exclaimed. Er, as a shop assistant, pet? Or on the till? 'No, as a model. I was a catwalk model for a few years and also did catalogue work and advertising. At the Aquascutum shows you had to take the coats off in a way that shows off the lining…' She stood up and gave me a demonstration. Ooh, vicar. 'It was good fun at the time, but it wasn't really me. It was the man who became my first husband, who was at Cambridge and played rugby. He persuaded me. I was very young...'

Goodness, just by lending her my coat I had discovered two things about her I did not know. What more is there to come? I asked myself.

After the meal, and almost two bottles of wine between us, I said she should stay the night as she had drunk too much to drive home. She thought about it for a moment and said okay then, thanks, but I'll stay in your spare bedroom. She had seen, on a tour of the cottage, that I have two spare bedrooms. It was, after all, just our first date – or second, I suppose, if you count the chance meeting at the book signing. She left first thing in the morning, as she had work to do, at an old folks' home in Ventnor.

A week later, I invited her to join me at a cocktail party in Newport given by the Mountbatten hospice charity. They had been the recipient of the charity prize at the Isle of Wight Book Awards and I had already met Nigel, the chief executive, and had invited him to my book launch. The cocktail party, a thank-you event for all those who had helped the Mountbatten, was chocka. I had not realised how big a charity it was, by far the biggest on the island, employing over 600 people plus volunteers.

We had a nice meal afterwards in Newport in a restaurant that was new to me. Handy having a local as a BF, able to introduce me to all the delights of the island I still had not discovered. She promised me lots of walks to hidden places. I hoped my legs would be up to them. But of course I did not say so. And then finally she invited me to her house for a meal and to stay the night. I had been longing for this. You can't truly, really, deeply know someone until you see them in their habitat: how they live, their décor and tastes, their style, their interests, their possessions. They are not just a reflection of how they live but who they are.

During our fifty-five years of marriage, even when we had no money, you and I always had colourful, unmatching crockery. It was always my standby if I could not think of a Christmas or birthday present for you. A couple of pretty, old-fashioned plates from a charity shop or second-hand shop were always acceptable. They were usually Portuguese, Italian, Spanish or old English Stoke pottery.

Miranda's house turned out to be a riot of colour and collections, of art and artifice, treasures she had found on the beach, most of which she had painted and turned into mirrors, shelves and ornaments. Her style reminded me a bit of my own office, which has about twenty collections, all crammed in... sorry, I mean artistically displayed. You were always complaining, refusing to clean it.

Her house is in a little terrace, on two floors, with two bedrooms. It's very narrow inside and outside: a narrow house with a narrow garden. I reckon the maximum width cannot be more than twelve feet. But it makes up for it in contents and the fact that it stretches a long way back, with a conservatory and rooms that have been converted at the back. The garden is unexpectedly long, divided into mini-gardens and courtyards, one leading into the other, with arches and trellises, statues and seats. Miranda has filled every corner with artworks and other treasures. There must be about five little garden areas, ending with her studio at the bottom of the garden.

Everything in the garden is Miranda's work: she laid the paths and built the little walls, mixed the concrete, fashioned patterns out of stone slabs, beach stones, pebbles, glass and shells. I was entranced. Apparently, she won an award a few years ago in a competition to find the best small gardens on the island and was presented with a prize by Alan Titchmarsh, no less. But then, five years ago, disaster struck: the whole garden was destroyed in a fire. It was really her fault. At the time she had an outdoor chiminea fire and one night she had not properly damped down all the embers before going to bed. The garden I was looking at now is a totally new creation, replacing the burned-down garden.

There was no sign of any pets, neither a dog nor a cat, which was a relief. I don't like to compete with animals for affection and attention. All that dog lovers – such as Caitlin and Jake – seem to do is fuss about or shout at their dogs and take them to the vet. At least Flora has not got a pet. I know dogs give you unconditional love, but they are such a responsibility, and restrict your freedom.

I raved about Miranda's house, how fascinating and unexpected it was, and she gave me a copy of a book that her sister Anabel had written and illustrated and published for Miranda's seventieth birthday – a children's story about a woman who lives in a tiny house with a tiny garden, full of treasures. It had been properly printed and was published in a limited edition. It reminded me of the lovely books that Caitlin creates for Davies family members on our birthdays.

Perhaps best of all, Miranda's house has a sea view from her bedroom window. From her bed she can see the yachts bobbing up and down, and in the distance, in good weather, so she said, she can clearly see the shore of the Solent, around Southampton. I had to put my specs on to see any ships. Lucky Miranda. I wish I had a sea view. I am in fact much nearer to the sea at Ryde than she is in Cowes – just three minutes away – but I can't actually see the sea from my house because of the houses opposite. Curses. Can't have everything in life.

Which of course is what I am trying to do.

And you will respond by saying that's what I always have

done, tried to get everything. And that I usually do get what I want.

Which of course I always denied and still would deny it. I maintain that most of the time I honestly don't know what I want. I just want to talk, consider the options, think of the alternatives, empty my thoughts. That's why I have missed talking to you so much these last seven years. I loved telling you things in my mind and in my life, even when you did not ask, wondering what I should do, which way to turn, what project to do, which event to go to, which invite to accept. You often sighed and said you were not going to indulge me because I knew all along what I wanted to do. And if you gave me advice I didn't like, I would ignore it anyway.

Will I get that with Miranda? Did she have it with her husbands? Yes, it turns out she has had two. The marriage to the first man did not last long. Then she married again, to a South African who was a keen sailor. In fact, they built a boat together.

I did not discover this until the following morning, after breakfast, when I was examining more of the paintings, objects, artworks and cuttings that decorated the walls of her house. I noticed a framed newspaper cutting, dating from the 1970s, from a local paper in Norfolk. It described how a young local couple were building a trimaran and planning to sail it across the Atlantic. The two of them were pictured together, cutting wood, creating the frame. I did not even know what a trimaran was. Turns out to be a three-hulled boat, as opposed to a catamaran, which has two. I could not believe it. So enterprising and clever. Building their own boat, from scratch, some thirty-nine feet long. It took them two years.

When it was all finished, they sailed the trimaran – the *Sweet Painted Lady* – to the Med. Then they crossed the Atlantic, going on to spend a further four years in the

Caribbean, sailing round all the islands, and to Miami. They slept on the boat, doing charter work on other vessels to make some money. They had no capital and were always hard up. Eventually, when she got pregnant, they returned to the Isle of Wight, where they settled down. Her husband worked as a yacht designer with Chay Blyth – famous for sailing round the world 'the wrong way' in 1970–71.

They had two sons but after another two years, the marriage ended. She stayed on the island, where she has now lived for forty years.

Later, she had a long relationship with a widower who lived in Portsmouth, which meant continually crossing the Solent, but he died a few years ago. Until now, she has been single, living on her own, though one of her sons – he is also a yacht designer – and his family live in the next street. She was not expecting to have another relationship. Which was roughly the same as me. I had tried, but had recently given up, deciding I would just be a lonely old widower, on my own, with lots of friends but no partner.

So will Miranda be my new partner? Will it last? We have got so far in such a short time. Well, we chat all the time. Seem to get on well. Have laughs. And both enjoy beach walks.

After that first visit to her house, I came home to Ryde and found myself thinking about her all the time. And about her promise to introduce me to all the parts of the island I did not know. At the moment, my new plan is to visit the island every two weeks to see her. Then, in between, she will come to see me in London. Train strikes permitting. She doesn't like to drive in London, and can't face motorways. I don't have a car, so that means both of us will be taking the train – from Southampton to Waterloo in her case and Waterloo to Portsmouth in mine, so I can catch the hovercraft to Ryde, which lands very near my house.

I am not sure I can face the logistics of all the travelling, and of being apart so often. I never thought I would end up with a girlfriend on the Isle of Wight. In my mind, if it ever happened, I assumed she would live in the London area. Which would be handy. And I would sell the Isle of Wight house.

I might try going via Southampton instead, and catching the Red Jet across the Solent, as that would be handier for Miranda's house near Cowes. Either way, the journey is rather hanging over me. I am afraid of missing a connection, or falling over, and no one knowing where I am. But I plan to have a go, as long as I can.

It's very exciting, this first stage in a new relationship. But a bit worrying, too. You know that neither of you has yet discovered the annoying aspects of the other's character. You are still on your best behaviour, showing your best side, not thinking about what might go wrong. Falling in love, as it is commonly called, does blind you. Yes, even at the age of eighty-six, that phrase passes through my ancient brain.

So far, Miranda seems warm and affectionate. We do have a bond, there is chemistry there. She is kind and caring. Probably quite emotional, in the nicest possible way, meaning she has empathy for those less fortunate than her. When she tells me about the people with dementia in the various homes she visits with her art therapy, and they suddenly remember a song or phrase from their childhood and their eyes light up, there are often tears in Miranda's eyes as she describes them.

I did worry at first that she might be a bit of a New Age hippie, away with the fairies, but there's not really much sign of that so far.

During her first visit to stay with me in London, by chance she met Jake and Rosa. They happened to call in with their new dog when Miranda was here last weekend. Jake did not ask any personal questions, did not want to know the details of our relationship. Which Caitlin and Flora will, when they eventually meet her.

I have shown them both photos of Miranda and her house and her artwork on my mobile – and they seemed to be impressed. And I also told them about her modelling career. They did not seem as fascinated by that as I am. I think they think my fascination with her modelling career, short though it was, is a bit creepy. I have explained that it is her experience in the sixties as a model, my decade, when I was there, that interests me. But they seemed happy that I appear to be happy. Which is what matters, I suppose.

I hope they will be pleased that Miranda has come into my life, someone to talk to and go places with. She is ten years younger than me, but I don't expect her to be my carer. That is not at all my object in having a lady friend. When the time comes, I will make my own arrangements and of course my three children and four grandchildren will be there when I need them.

I have not met any of Miranda's family yet, the son and her grandchildren who live in the next street. Her other son is a shipwright living in Australia, and has no children. Her three grandsons are much younger than my granddaughters – seven, five and three. I like kids that age. They still like silly jokes and doing stupid things. Whereas Amarisse and Sienna, now they are teenagers, are getting a bit old for my idea of fun.

I suppose the only problem so far with our relationship is the travelling to and fro between London and the Isle of Wight, which will get harder and more tiring with age. Because of the travelling, I had been thinking this last year, when I was on my own, that I might sell the Isle of Wight house or rent it out.

Will I be going back and forth to the island to see Miranda when I am ninety? Will I be up to going anywhere? Will she want to be lumbered with an old git who needs help to put his shoes on and get across the road? She seems fit and healthy, but you never know, she might fade before me.

Ah well. Live for today. That's what I have always done, as you well know. Count your blessings. All of us lucky enough to be still alive have to remind ourselves of that...

So what's your guess? What do you think is going to happen, oh wise one?

LETTER SEVENTEEN

*Margaret on a crumbling dry-stone wall in one of
our fields at Loweswater.*

Up the Spurs

Hello there. Do calm down, all will be revealed...

I suppose I rather ran Miranda off her feet, considering I had only just met her. I was already making arrangements, making plans for the future, before I had properly got to know her. But at my age you can't muck around, wasting time – I might not be here next week. So, after my stay at her house on the island, she came to London for a longer weekend, during which I walked her over the Heath to Hampstead, and then to Highgate, and back through Waterlow Park. Highgate Cemetery and Karl Marx's grave was closed. We will do it in the spring, I said, blithely.

After that I went to see her again on the Isle of Wight, and then she came to London to stay with me for six days. I had two events lined up, the sort I always like to go to with someone, so we can discuss it all afterwards and make catty comments. For the last year, I have tended not to accept evening invites if it means trailing somewhere all on my own.

The first event was at the British Library. You will remember decades ago I gave them my collection of original handwritten Beatles lyrics, still on show in the Manuscript Room, next to Magna Carta, where our dear late Queen admired them. I have now finally handed over the last of my Beatles rubbish – sorry, treasures – but my room is still chocka with stuff I have collected. I do worry that, if I suddenly pop my clogs, none of the kids will know what or where everything is, any more than you would have done. I fear they might bin things without knowing what they are, or get in some chancer who will offer them a tenner to clear the whole room, without them realising that some items in my collections are worth thousands... Or so I fondly imagine.

I still have first editions of newspapers and magazines, including the first copy of *Private Eye*, which I reckon is worth £5k. Then there's my London Underground maps, which I mentioned earlier, including original artwork by Harry Beck, the creator of the iconic London Tube map. And my suffragette material. I have someone from Bonhams coming soon to look at what I have left and value it. I will spend the money on taking Miranda first class to the West Indies. If she is lucky.

The Beatles stuff I have just handed over to the British Library contains notebooks, research material, photos, early press releases – these were worth nothing all those years ago, but now anything to do with the Beatles has a value. I even gave them that Super 8 cine film I did of Paul and Linda coming to visit us in Portugal in 1968. The British Library had asked me to come and give a talk about the material and show the film, so I invited Miranda to come with me. Living on the Isle of Wight for forty years, she does not get a lot of metropolitan fun. I took her down to the BL on the 214 bus – I'm far too tight to pay for a taxi, and anyway, the bus stop is only two minutes away from my front door. The bus came at once, so we arrived early, and I suggested we take a walk round the newly refurbished and magnificent St Pancras station. Miranda had never seen it before, and she was most impressed. The Christmas lights were up, and the station was full of family groups and couples hand in hand, all heading for Eurostar to take them to Paris for the weekend. The shops were gleaming and glittering, more upmarket than I remembered.

There is now even a branch of Fortnum & Mason. The arches and architecture and brickwork are of course stunning, since it has all been cleaned up. Miranda loved it – she is such an enthusiast and so appreciative. With her art college training, she knows more about design than I do.

The BL event went well, all tickets sold. They streamed it so people could watch it at home, live. I answered questions afterwards, some of which came from places like Texas and Toronto, folks sitting at home, 10,000 miles away, and talking to me. Amazing. Afterwards, I splashed out on a late supper – no expense spared – at Pizza Express across from the BL on Euston Road.

The next day brought yet more excitement. The week before, I had received a call from someone called Steve at Tottenham Hotspur, who was ringing to offer me his congratulations. When I asked him 'Congratulations on what, exactly?', Steve told me it was fifty years ago this week that my book *The Glory Game* came out. I had not realised, though I know it is still in print in lots of different countries – surprisingly, perhaps, as it is about a north London football team whose players I spent a year with, all those decades ago, in the dressing room and on the training ground. Most of the players are long forgotten and football has changed out of all recognition in the intervening years, but I still get letters about the book. Students at colleges around the world want to use some of the forty pages of surveys I shoved in at the end – mostly because I was not able to work them into the book itself. No one since has been able to get access to a group of top sportsmen in quite the same way. None of the players at the time had agents, managers, brand managers, lawyers, accountants, personal security, which all Premier League players have today.

I was busy when Steve rang, trying to finish a column, so

didn't catch his surname or listen properly to what he was proposing. I thought perhaps it was a wind-up, some Gooner friend trying to be funny. But three days later he sent me a long email setting out the details. He was inviting me to come to the Spurs game on Saturday, a home fixture against Leeds United, bring a guest, have lunch, sit in the best seats for the game, and then be interviewed at half-time on the pitch. I asked if there would be any chance of my bringing two guests. Steve said he could fix it. So I invited Jake. He has a season ticket anyway, which I passed on to him when I gave up going regularly. (It became such a faff getting there at my age on public transport, and the games are all usually on the telly anyway.) But the real reason I wanted him to come was so he could drive the three of us to the ground. The new Tottenham Hotspur Stadium, I explained to Miranda, is a state-of-the-art design, holds nearly 63,000 spectators, and is generally amazing. She was suitably impressed. Her only football experience so far was when Rich, her boyfriend who died, took her to watch Pompey. Come on, you know what team that is. It's Portsmouth. You are a football expert, remember, despite never going to games.

We had a grand day out, with a lovely lunch. Jake found an excellent place to park and Spurs won in the last minute. At half-time, I did my piece to camera. And I told a rather rude story. Usually, the celeb guests on the pitch at half-time are famous former players or some well-known actor who is a Spurs fan. I remember Warren Mitchell (Alf Garnett) and Leslie Phillips, the *Carry On* star, being interviewed at half-time on the pitch.

I was told they would also try to invite one of the players from the 1972 team, the one I wrote about in *The Glory Game*. That player turned out to be Terry Naylor. He was never a star player, but he was in the first team pool. Later, when he retired, he became a postman. Imagine that happening today. Any Premier League player, even a journeyman, is earning £100k a week these days – while the top stars get £400k per week. They can all now retire as multimillionaires.

The interviewer asked me about *The Glory Game*, and how I came to write it. Then I went on to tell them that, when I was travelling with the team, I used to amuse them by asking questions about the players. I had been to their homes, met their wives, interviewed them all one to one, without the other players around to listen in and mock. Then, on the train or bus home after a game, I would ask the team questions about their fellow players, such as who voted Labour in the last election? The answer was Steve Perryman – he was the only one who did. Which player has a share in a fish and chip shop? Cyril Knowles. I also asked, just to amuse them, which player has the biggest willy?

There was a gasp from the announcer doing the interview at the Tottenham Hotspur Stadium. He immediately put his hand to his mouth, saying he would now be sacked. I sensed that many of the 63,000 in the stadium watching and listening on the big screens were a bit surprised as well. During the course of the 1971–72 season, I had been constantly in the dressing room and was accustomed to seeing them all naked. Back in 1972, when I asked that question, the players all said Martin Chivers, he must be the most well-endowed, as he was so big and strong. But the best-endowed player, from my observations, was not the six-foot striker Chivers but a rather thin, lanky defender, who – fifty years later – was now standing beside me on the pitch. 'And the winner of my little childish competition,' I said, pointing to Terry, 'was the one and only... Terry Naylor.'

The joke went viral. People in the ground watching on the big screen caught it on their mobile and posted it on Twitter (or should that be X?) and Facebook and elsewhere. Both Caitlin and Flora, who had no idea I was at the ground, were bombarded by friends forwarding it to them, with no indication of the context in which I'd made the joke, of course. How childish, they both said to me later in messages, telling some story about willies, at your age. How on earth had I come to say that? I said it was a long story and I would tell them when I next saw them. But I have still have not got round to it.

After the game, Miranda and I, along with Jake and Rosa, had a lovely supper at Ruby's studio flat in Crouch End. She had roasted two chickens. And cooked lots of veggie dishes. Wasn't that lovely? Having a granddaughter making a meal for five, especially when you consider the size of her kitchen. You never got to see it, alas; but believe me, it's titchy.

Miranda loved staying at my house and raved about the paintings that you and I collected – most of them by women, including Vanessa Bell, Beryl Cook, Mary Fedden and Helen Bradley. The décor is rather battered these days, but still colourful, as you created it. She also raved about my garden, which surprised me – as her own garden is absolutely amazing. She thought a lot of the features of my garden were very like her own – bowers, seats, arches, statues, objects and little hidden corners. Yes, I have changed it a bit since you were here. You would now think it is too cluttered. Miranda was very sad not to see Tortee. She – I mean he – had just gone to sleep for the winter.

One evening, when I was making the supper, Miranda went out into the garden to do some clearing up of the fallen leaves. I had been putting off doing it as my back and shoulders were playing up. It was dark when she eventually came back inside, and I gave her a drink. I told her to sit down in the front room by the fire and not come into the kitchen and watch me cooking. I am rather a domestic god these days and always cook the supper when I entertain visitors. It was a special potato and back bacon dish. I got the recipe from a doctor friend in Bequia.

Then I sat down with Miranda in the front room with a drink and some smoked salmon sandwiches. 'While I was doing the leaves,' she said, 'I got talking to a little robin. It fluttered down right beside me and watched me clearing the leaves, hoping I would unearth some grubs for him. So sweet. It stood right at my feet and we had a good chat...' 'Oh yeah,' I said. 'I know those robins. We have a family of them in the garden, year after year. They sit in the bush on the left, watching everything.'

Miranda went on, 'And then I talked to Margaret...' You what? 'Yes, Margaret told me she was pleased to see me in the garden, and obviously enjoying it. Then she said she was happy I was happy with Hunter – and that he was happy with me.' You what? I asked again. This is the part of Miranda's character that appears to be off with the fairies. Okay then, super sensitive. Earlier that day, while we were walking on the Heath, she had gone to look closer under the hanging branches of a beech tree in full autumn colours, a blaze of orange and red, one of those huge ones beside the open grassland where the police horses used to train. I went to look where she had gone and found her under the tree in tears. The beauty of it had made her emotional.

I don't think you and me, being northerners, would ever react quite like that, beautiful though nature can be. But Miranda had clearly felt your presence in the garden, so who am I to mock?

'Did Margaret do a lot of gardening?' asked Miranda. 'I wondered which plants she had planted. Perhaps next time she speaks to me I could ask her which ones she had chosen...'

I explained to her that you had done nothing in the garden. I had always done everything. And I had to learn to do so from scratch, whereas you had been brought up in a gardening family – your dad, Arthur, was a passionate gardener. You never even cut the lawn, far less planned anything. But I added that you did enjoy our garden, sat in it a lot, and appreciated what I had done, especially in our spring garden, with all its bulbs and blossom.

I then told Miranda that half of your ashes are under the summerhouse, right beside where she was sweeping up the leaves. So possibly she had picked up your presence, your essence, and was communing spiritually with you. That was why she had imagined she had seen the ghost of Margaret Forster. And had talked to you.

Miranda, I am beginning to learn, can be a bit emotional. I'm not used to that. Will I be able to cope?

Eee, worra lass, eh?

LETTER EIGHTEEN

In our garden at Loweswater, 1990s.

Our First Row

Hi, hen.

So how is it going with Miranda, you ask? Well, I am sure you have at least been wondering about the latest situation. You'd better come a bit closer, this is for your ears only.

We have just had our first row, of a sort. Not bad, I suppose, as it is now three months since we first met, during which time we have done so many things and been to so many places. This is what happens when you have a new partner in old age. You experience so much in such a short time. You learn about her life, her family, her children, her house, her interests, her character – just as she learns about you.

You are also in such a hurry, fearing this won't last, can't last, telling yourself you are so lucky to have met someone so compatible at this late stage. How long will it go on, you wonder? You're not expecting that you will fall out, or at least you hope not, but at eighty-six and seventy-six, one or both of us is bound to be fading soon – and it's more likely to be me, being ten years older. Miranda does seem to be very fit; she can walk for miles and carry enormously heavy rucksacks and bags. I get her to carry all my stuff, even my phone, when we are out walking. Yes, very lazy, I know. But you will remember that I was always like that. Such weak arms, I could carry nowt. When we were youth hostelling, you were the pit pony.

Are women naturally heavy lifters? Generations of humping

out washing and hanging it up, bringing home shopping, making beds – God, I find that absolutely knackering – and of course carrying babies around, inside them at first and then on their hips or in their arms. Poor things. How do they survive it?

You have missed most of the 'woke' controversy, by the way. It would be too boring to explain in detail, but 'woke' is something to do with being fully awake to injustices and inequalities like racism and sexism. Millennials and members of Generation Z seem to be more exercised by it than baby boomers. I am always getting told off by Flora for making remarks that I think are just playful but she thinks are sexist. When writing my columns, I have to beware jokes that could rebound on me. Good job I don't do any social media. Most columnists get hammered all the time by their readers. I don't do Twitter (or X), Facebook or whatever, so I never know what reactions there are from readers to my *Sunday Times* Money column or *Saga* column. My *New Statesman* column is safer as it is about football. Probably just as well I don't read any feedback – I've been repeating the same old stuff in my columns for twenty-six years now.

Miranda has just been staying again for a week and I got her to do lots of jobs, including going out on the first-floor balcony to give it a good scrubbing. It gets so filthy every winter with dead leaves and peeling paint everywhere. You will remember the balcony, in my room, only a couple of feet wide, through the tall double windows. You have to crouch to get through the window as it has been sticking for decades. There are a few cracks in the balcony and, as I pushed her out, Miranda was worried that it might collapse. I used to go out and clean it every autumn but now I can't bend down to get out of the window. Just as I can't get up on the roof as I used to. Which reminds me. We had a roof leak a while back on the top floor, in my lodger Denise's bedroom. I got a handyman to go up on the roof and seal it. He said he would come back to do a second coat, but the weather has been awful ever since.

I do miss being able to do basic domestic repairs. I know I am a bodge-jobber, and awfully slipshod, but over the last sixty years in this house I was able to sort most of the leaks and blocked drains we had here. It's annoying always having to ask for help. It is one of the things about old age that really upsets me. I feel so useless. Not even being able to move the sofa.

Anyway, Miranda did a grand job. She scrubbed the front downstairs window shelf as well. And cleared up the leaves and grass cuttings from the lawn. I gave it what I hope will be the last cutting of the year, with the electric hover mower. That's easy – I can still do that.

She asks constantly about the tortoise, what he is doing, where he is sleeping. Miranda came into my life after Tortee had gone to sleep for the winter, so she half suspects he is an imaginary tortoise. I have told her that he is now at least fifty-five years old. Have I made that up? Can you remember? I know we bought him from that pet shop in Camden Town, now long gone. Palmers, I think it was called. It was after either Caitlin or Jake had been born, so back in the sixties. He has outlived you and will probably outlive me as well.

Today, the last day of Miranda's week here before she returns to the Isle of Wight, we sat down at the kitchen table to have a meeting. A meeting about her book. When I first met her, back in September, I was fascinated by her life, what she had done, from being a catwalk model to sailing across the Atlantic. I asked, had she ever thought of writing her memoirs? It turned out that for most of her adult life she has been scribbling down little stories, scenes and poems for her own amusement. At school, the teachers apparently treated her as if she was stupid and never encouraged her creative talents. Why not try to write your own life story, I suggested. So many people do these days. Self-publishing is now easy and not too expensive. Keep it simple, write it in chronological order, don't jump ahead to events that have not happened yet, and don't start philosophising before we know who you are or what you have done. And avoid purple prose or anything mystical and spiritual. I had enough trouble with George Harrison when I did the Beatles biography. He wanted to talk about India most of the time.

She has been working on her memoirs for the last three months. I have read the first five chapters – and really liked them. She has a literary touch and is good on narrative. The first five chapters cover her boarding school years from the age of seven. There have been enough books telling us what hell that could be, the abuse and horrors and neglect, but I found it riveting. Poor lass. It must have been like losing your parents, being sent away to school at such a young age.

She has often mentioned her time at boarding school, and how it did little for her confidence. Come on, I said, I thought the whole point of boarding school was to instil confidence. You do, after all, have quite a posh voice and appear pretty self-assured. That is meaningless, she said. The teachers humiliated her, did nothing to encourage her interest in poetry and art, put her down all the time, did not understand her. She felt she didn't fit in. And she was useless at exams. It scarred her for life, or so she believes. And she also believes that her book will be no good.

I said I thought her first five chapters *were* good, that she *did* have talent, and that she must continue. 'There is much more in your life than your awful schooldays, such as being a model and sailing the Caribbean. Readers will find that fascinating.' So I encouraged her to continue. But I warned her that a proper publisher will not be interested in an unknown. And an agent wouldn't take her on either. They are all bastards. You have to be someone really famous, like a TV chef, a reality TV star or an Influencer, before an agent will get out of bed.

I promised her that when she had finished, I would read the whole thing and then help her self-publish. I know she has no savings and that sales of her artwork are very up and down. She does have a job – working in old people's homes – but that pays her only £25 an hour. I said we could get 100 copies published – it won't cost much – enough for you to give copies to your family and close friends. I am sure the Cowes bookshop, where we first met, whose owner and manager we both know, will take a few copies on sale or return. Local bookshops do try to help local authors. And Isle of Wight newspapers and magazines are bound to review it.

You reach a certain stage in your life when you want to capture it all, I said, and write it all down as a record for posterity – a kind of proof that you existed – so that the generations of your family to come will know who you were. I also told her it would be fun to do her memoirs, and rather therapeutic to look back, wonder why she had done certain things and gone to certain places, and to remember both the happy times and the not-so-happy ones.

For the past three months, Miranda seems to have been talking about her book non-stop. She's enjoying the writing well enough, but is worried about the grammar, the layout, the cover, the title, and about how long it should be. She's got techie friends of hers to read it and offer advice. I told her that most authors are like that. They are obsessed by their book, but afraid it might turn out to be boring and hopeless. It is normal. You just have to bash on. When you get stuck or bored, just start a new chapter. But the important thing is to get it written, and not to worry at this stage about making it perfect. And, please, I said, I really don't want to read any more until you have finished the whole thing. What I have read so far is great. Honest.

Do you remember back in 1966 when I started my first novel? You had already had your first book published. I felt so nervous and worried about trying to do a whole book. So far I had just been a journalist, writing mostly 500-word pieces. So I remember how daunting it was embarking on 80,000 words. The task seemed beyond me. It was as if I had trained all my life for the 100 metres – and now had to run the marathon.

Please help, I said to you, back in the sixties. Please read this chapter. Please, please. You said no. You rotter. Just this one page, please? I will be your best friend. You still refused, saying you would not read one word – until I had finished the whole book. If I really wanted to write a book, I would have to do it all on my own.

You, of course, were always an unusual author. You did not like showing anyone what you had written, or even discussing it. With novels especially, you would deny you were working on one. If the children barged in on you, you said you were just playing. You wrote it all in fountain pen, in your immaculate handwriting. At the end of each day, or the beginning of the next session, you did not read what you had written or number the pages. You did no corrections or rewrites while you were writing your novels. Only at the end did you number the pages and read it through, to make sure you had not changed a woman's name or given her different-coloured hair. Then you parcelled it up – your only copy – and posted it to your typist.

But your non-fiction was different. When you were writing non-fiction you behaved like a normal author, thinking about it all the time and talking about it non-stop. That is what

I remember about you in your writing life. Every author, of course, is slightly different.

What I did not know when I encouraged Miranda to start writing was that she does not use a computer programme such as Word. What she has been doing on her laptop these last few months is writing her book in an endless series of emails, or handwriting chunks on scraps of paper, then paying a friend to put all the bits together, work out what goes where, and put it into chapters using proper word-processing software. This week she brought with her another six chapters, which her friend has captured and Miranda has printed out. I agreed to read them, though really I would rather have waited until the very end.

So today, at the kitchen table, I went through them, making marks, suggesting changes. Not because I am a good critic, which I am not, or good on spelling, or a literary person – which both you and Caitlin are – but I have been at this game a long time. For years I was an editor on various *Sunday Times* sections, so am used to reading and correcting copy, knocking it into shape so the reader will read on.

It then also came out that Miranda had not only got help to put her material in Word, but that she has been in touch with a freelance sub editor about correcting her grammar and punctuation in the chapters she has written so far. I told her it was a daft idea. 'Your English is fine! Save your pennies.' There is no point in doing correcting and sub editing now, not until it is all finished and up on the screen. *Then* you yourself can go through it, correcting and polishing. I had not realised that Miranda is even less of a techie than me. She can't cut and paste, does not know how to enlarge or change the typeface. So she has been getting in a mess and panicking because she does not understand the process of making a book.

You will sympathise with Miranda in this, as you could not

use a typewriter or a computer. But at least you could afford to have all your stuff professionally typed and presented.

At this point I must have said something hurtful. Maybe suggested that by her age she could have found a computer class for the elderly. They must have them in Cowes.

I clearly overdid my criticism. And she burst into tears. She said I did not understand. She had no confidence, she did not understand modern technology, was useless and stupid. Her teachers were right.

Oh God, what have I done? It's not as if I am even a half-decent techie myself. I have all the gear but only know what I know. I scream at my computer all the time, lose things, go mad when they update. I had to teach myself typing when I started on the *Manchester Evening Chronicle* back in 1958. I still do two-finger typing, full of mistakes and rubbish, but I can write rubbish rather quickly. Then I go through it again more slowly, correcting and polishing.

Anyway, I apologised, said I was sorry. I had not meant to criticise her, just to make a few helpful suggestions. She then went off for a walk on her own on the Heath, and came back with a large box of strawberries from a shop I never go to as it is so expensive.

So we kissed and made up.

I know I can be a bit bossy. The children tell me that. I am always saying to them 'this is what you should do'. I have got worse with age, I suppose, always convinced I am right. When Jake comes round to do some gardening, he will not do it if I am standing over him. I have to go indoors, leave him to it, otherwise I will just interfere.

So Miranda is finding out what I am like. And I am finding out what she is like.

I have invited her to come with me to the West Indies in January. I have booked it all up. Paid the fares and the hotel deposits. Will we find more things we did not know about each other in Bequia? Being together for three weeks will be our longest spell together so far. Will we irritate each other? Or will it be happiness all the way? That's if we get through Christmas without any further upsets... Miranda will be with her family and I am going to be with Caitlin at her new bungalow for our family Christmas. So we won't be together all the time, which might be a relief.

I took Miranda to the bus stop this morning, the first stage of her journey back to the Isle of Wight. She happened to mention that she has an appointment with her GP this coming week. Oh, what for, pet? She thinks she has a hernia. It's been rumbling away for a year or so, but it has been especially bad this week. And there was me boasting how fit she is, that she is far fitter than me, never seems to be ill, has never had any operations...

On the other hand, she added, it might not be a hernia. It might be something more serious. She might need a hysterectomy... I said I had heard it can be a painful procedure and can take a long time to recover from. You were lucky not to have to go through it. But then you had more than enough health problems to worry about.

Will we ever make it to the West Indies?

Oh God, love in old age... The love bit is marvellous, but it's hard to ignore the bits that come to us all in old age...

Fingers crossed. Keep the heed, Hunter.

LETTER NINETEEN

*Margaret at home in London. A good professional
shot by a photographer who lived nearby.*

A Trip to A&E

How do, how are you? And how am I? Don't ask…

Although Miranda and I were not going to be together for the actual Christmas festivities, we decided to have the last week before Christmas together, shuttling between my cottage in Ryde and hers in Gurnard. But it was agreed that, after Christmas, she would come to London on 7 January for my eighty-seventh birthday, and then of course on 18 January we would be off to the West Indies. Hurrah!

On my birthday – which I also share with Amarisse – Miranda would meet all my family for the first time. So far she had just met Jake and Rosa, Richard, and Ruby. But not Caitlin and Flora – in a way the vital ones, being my dear darling daughters, with beady eyes and reprimands at the ready…

So, we had three days together at my Ryde house and then, on the morning of Sunday 18 December, we set off for Miranda's house. Oh, I remember the date well. How could I not? It was the day of the 2022 World Cup Final in Qatar, France versus Argentina. I was looking forward to it soooo much.

Miranda had agreed to watch it with me at her house, on her telly, which is about the size of a postage stamp. She had watched several games while she was staying at my house, which was good of her, and I had been kindly instructing her about the finer points of corners and free kicks. But not the off-side rule. That is graduate study. I assured her the final would be spectacular, a footballing showpiece. Messi will either become an all-time Argentine hero or once again disappoint his nation. And just wait till you see him. He is small and weedy. You won't believe he is a football superstar.

We left my house around 10.30, saying cheerio to my friends in the street, Denise and Neil, asking them to put my bins out, as I did not expect to be back till sometime in the New Year. Halfway across the island in Miranda's car, I suddenly had the most appalling pains in my stomach. I got Miranda to stop the car and find a chemist and get some Rennies, thinking it might be indigestion. Fat chance.

By this time the pains were constant, and I was doubled up and screaming. Clearly it was not indigestion, but I had no idea what it was. I felt my stomach was going to explode. The fact that the pain was constant, not in waves, was strange. I had never had such pains before. Was it a burst appendix? A hernia? With all the health things I worry about in my life, such as my heart and my arthritis, I had not got round to fretting about what goes on lower down: stomach and liver and prostate and all that. I have had quite enough to worry about.

At Miranda's house, I went to bed with a hot-water bottle on my belly. After an hour, I felt worse, so she rang for an ambulance. I had to answer lots of questions twice and was told the waiting time was two hours.

The festive season is never a good time to be poorly, but this year we had an economic crisis, rail strikes, the NHS strikes, though fortunately on the Isle of Wight the nurses were working. We decided instead to drive to A&E – where the waiting time was six hours. I had never been to St Mary's – the Isle of Wight hospital in Newport – since I bought the house two years ago. Nor even registered with a local GP. Very remiss of me, with my history.

We queued up at reception in A&E and managed to find the last two seats. It was a mass of heaving, groaning, pathetic, miserable-looking humanity. Just like me. There was a young bloke beside me with his mother. His hand was bloodied, as if he had picked a fight with a glass door. Behind us was another young man with blood on his chest, shouting and screaming in agony. He appeared to be with his wife or girlfriend. Both the women had bleached hair and looked thin and deprived.

The one with the injured hand was on his mobile, telling someone that a fucking nutter was screaming and shouting behind him. The wife / girlfriend of the shouting man got up and rushed at the bloke on the phone. Who are you calling a fucking nutter? The two blokes exchanged punches. And then the women joined in.

It was all so sudden and surprising. And yet so theatrical, as if it had been choreographed. We watched in horror. It did at least take my mind off my own groans and moans. Until Security arrived to drag them apart and settle them down.

My pains were still there and I was doubled up, probably making as much noise as the nutter. I wondered if I would pass out before I was seen. Reception had told us the normal bed capacity in A&E at St Mary's was twenty-six – but they already had seventy waiting for a bed. Oh God. What a time to choose to be unwell.

I noticed a TV screen beside the reception desk. Go on, I said to Miranda, ask if they can get the football. She went over and the whole waiting room heard the reply. 'This is a hospital. Not a hotel.' Oh, the shame.

Eventually, I reached the triage stage, whatever that means, was passed around from little room to little room, had my blood pressure checked, and my temperature taken, all the usual boring stuff I know they have to do when all you really want is some heavy-duty painkiller, at once. I got Miranda to plead with a friendly-looking nurse for some morphine. She said she would ask a doctor – and then disappeared, not to be seen again.

All hospital A&E departments are like this these days, especially at weekends and at Christmas. Hard to believe that just two years ago, at the height of the Covid pandemic, we were all out in the streets clapping the wonderful staff of the NHS. The staff themselves are now leaving in droves. I noticed that the names being called out were all old-fashioned English surnames. When I go to the Royal Free in London, for a clinic or a blood test, so many of the names seem to be foreign. Not surprising in cosmopolitan London. And of course, in London, all around there are people speaking foreign languages – with children and grandchildren having to translate for the older generation. The Isle of Wight is an isolated Brit island that never had immigrant communities.

After what seemed like hours, and even more tests, I got to see an actual doctor. He promised me morphine, which a nurse eventually brought. I was then suddenly dumped on a trolley and wheeled into a long corridor and left there. I felt pleased that at last I'd been attended to. Even if I now seemed to have been forgotten again.

After a couple of hours, and again just as suddenly, I found myself being transferred to a proper bed and wheeled by a porter down a long corridor. No idea where I was going, or why. I was left in the corner of a room that felt strangely familiar. Uniformed nurses were bustling around, moving beds and screens into the room. I realised I was back in the A&E waiting room where several hours earlier I had witnessed the fight. All the waiting-room chairs and furniture had been taken out, but the reception desk was still there, and the TV set still blank. The nurses were turning the waiting room into an extra ten-bed hospital ward and they were busy pushing and dragging in the beds.

I watched with fascination as they completed the transformation, right in front of my eyes. It reminded me of a play I once saw in the West End where they kept the curtain open during the interval so you could watch the stagehands moving the sets around, getting the stage ready for the next scene. I remember thinking this is much better than the actual play. A woman in civilian clothes seemed to be supervising the transformation. When next she passed my bed, directing the stagehands, I asked if she was management. She said certainly not. No nurse these days wants to be mistaken for management. They are the baddies. She said she was Head of Nursing. She had been at home, having done her shift for the day, when she was called back urgently to the hospital to turn the A&E waiting room into a ward. She had not had time to put on her uniform and had come in as she was. She turned out to be from Brazil. So, naturally, I spoke fluent kitchen Portuguese to her, sympathising with her on Brazil's exit from the World Cup.

Later that evening, I was moved to yet another ward. The porter told me I was in luck – I was now going to a classy ward, for emergency surgical patients. I had an ultrasound scan, was given painkillers and was linked up to assorted drips for what seemed like hours.

The consultant eventually came around late in the evening with his entourage, and I hoped he would explain what was wrong with me. He asked cheerily how I was. I moaned, then managed a smile to say the worst part was that I had missed the World Cup Final. Oh, it was brilliant, he said. Especially the last ten minutes. I wondered how he had managed to watch it. Lucky beggar.

His diagnosis was gallbladder stones. Me neither. I didn't

know where they are or what they do. But of course I have heard stories about them being one of the most painful conditions that anyone can have. Which had turned out to be true. Fortunately, the constant stomach pains were now less severe, thanks to all the painkillers, oxygen and drips. But turning over in bed was impossible – the slightest movement was agony. Getting out of bed was beyond me so I had to ask for a bed pan. But I was too late. I started wetting myself. Oh God, how embarrassing.

The consultant's team of young, attentive doctors and nurses, some making notes, were all looking very serious and straight-faced. The consultant was quite relaxed and friendly. He explained roughly where the gallbladder was and what its function was. I asked why the stones had formed but it seems there is no one cause. It can happen at any time, at any age, to both men and women. Women particularly seem to suffer badly.

He explained there were two types of surgery they could do – a full operation to open me up and remove the gallbladder, or keyhole surgery. He declared that he did not really want to operate at all. Because of my age and condition and medical history. Cheeky sod. I had of course had to tell them about my triple heart bypass five years ago, and my arthritis, and new knee, and other excitements. He already knew my age – almost eighty-seven. If I get there, next month, I said. He laughed. He was sure I would get there. I spent four horrendous nights in that ward, hearing shouts and screams all night long and the constant bleeps and sounds of the heart monitors. But the really awful pains seemed to have subsided, thanks to all the drugs I had been given. I was let out on the fifth day, but had to come back two days later to have blood tests and be officially discharged. I am sure they were glad to have my bed for one of the waiting horde.

Back at Miranda's house, I stayed in bed for the next few days, entirely shattered. I had lost my appetite and felt awful. I could not put on my socks and shoes or get out of bed unaided. After three days, when I felt a bit better, she drove me across the island and I returned to my own house.

Caitlin, Jake and Flora had been in constant contact – mainly with Miranda, as my fingers were not up to answering my mobile – and they were clearly very worried about their poor dad. I was not supposed to be on my own, so they had decided between themselves to take turns to come and stay with me and give Miranda a break, thus ruining their own Christmas plans and giving themselves a hell of a journey. Travelling to the Isle of Wight is awkward at any time, not just at Christmas. Miranda had been doing everything for me so far, but she had her own family who she needed to be with at Christmas.

Jake came first, and stayed with me for three days, thereby missing the family Christmas at Caitlin's at the seaside. The moment he arrived, I got him to turn my TV on. I can never remember how it works. Jake managed to find me the World Cup Final on catch-up. And yes, it was brilliant, all the way through, as the consultant had told me.

I always find football relaxing. I don't watch anything else on TV. I'm not up to working out what is going on in TV dramas. You will remember how, when I occasionally watched plays with you, I was constantly asking, is it a flashback? who are these people? why should I be interested in them? But I can totally immerse myself in football. I tell myself that when I am old, much older than I am today, I will do nothing but watch football all day long and drink wine, till I pass out. I won't go that way, of course. Something mundane will get me, like being run over by a bus while jaywalking across Highgate Road. But now I expect it will be my gallbladder that explodes and finishes me off. Could be Messi. I mean messy.

Fans say the 2022 World Cup Final was the best ever. I have always said the 1966 final was better. I know, I was there, so just belt up. But now I will remember the day of the 2022 final forever. For what happened to me that day on the Isle of Wight.

Jake made Christmas lunch for me. He cooked sea bass, as I had been told I could not have fats of any sort. And Miranda was able to join us. Her family Christmas lunch had been held on Christmas Eve. It was probably the most unusual Christmas lunch I have ever had. I did not drink any alcohol – just tonic water, which I hate – as I had been told not to drink.

But Jake got through the bottle of Fleurie he had bought me for my Christmas present.

Caitlin came to stay with me next. She was very tough and made sure I did not drink any wine. Not even mixed with tonic water.

Then, alas, after Christmas, after Jake and Caitlin had gone home, the same thing happened again. The hellish pains returned. Worse than ever. Miranda had to take me to A&E and we went through the whole palaver again. My friendly consultant had now gone. It turned out he had been seconded from University Hospital Southampton to help out during emergencies. I was in hospital for most of a week, during which I was seen by four different doctors, mostly saying different things. I was eventually discharged with a sackful of pills, one of which was going to dissolve the gallstones. I would need to stay on them for three months.

Eventually, Flora managed to get on a car ferry to the island. She stayed with me at Ryde for three nights, and then drove me back to London with Miranda, who was going to stay with me until I felt better.

I was still feeling groggy when I got home. I could never have made it back to London via my usual route – hovercraft, bus, train, Tube, bus. So, thank goodness for Flora driving all that way, and then back.

Sorry to have to tell you all this. I am boring myself going over it all. You have been through far worse. I made a vow several years ago never to discuss my health with anyone younger than me. But you are my age – well, two years younger than me, in fact, so round about the same age as me – so hard cheese. The young don't want to hear about operations. What do you expect, at your age? – you can tell that's what they are thinking. But old people are always willing to listen to other old timers droning on about their hospital sagas – in fact, they are just waiting for a pause in the story so they can start to drone on about their own.

You never wanted to talk about your latest treatments, with anyone. Until the very end, you kept them private. You tried never to tell even close friends when your next appointment was as you did not want them fussing and going on about it. How are you? Poor you, and so on and so on. I suppose you did not want sympathy. Whereas I love sympathy.

In this modern age of mobiles and emails, the more people you tell, the more they contact you. Which is kind, I suppose. But even I can get fed up having to tell people how I am. So please don't go around Heaven blabbing about the poorly time your old husband is having down there. I don't want any calls.

I am fine, thank you very much. At least I am still here.

In a way, you were fortunate, just having one thing wrong with you for all those years. Bad-taste remark, I know. Fifty years with cancer is not nothing. What I mean is that you were always so healthy otherwise. You did not have arthritis, dementia, deteriorating eyesight, shingles, depression, the way your mother had. You always appeared so fit and strong – walking for miles, up and down fells. You glowed. And of course, you never moaned.

I remember, when I first met you, thinking I am looking forward to seeing Margaret when she is an old woman. She is bound to be rosy-cheeked, while I will be a wrinkled old wreck. My old body has taken a battering these last few years with so many different things going wrong. Let me count the ways I have been chopped up. Okay, I will let you off. It was a joke.

I can't help wondering what's going to happen next... But first I have to get to the bottom of this gallbladder business. I never knew I had one, and now it has taken over my life. What am I going to do about the problem? Will it return? Can I do anything about it?

Try not to panic, Hunter.

LETTER TWENTY

Margaret in our conservatory at Loweswater.

2023
Happy Birthday, Hunt

Thanks for all the lovely presents you gave me over the years – six decades' worth.

I managed to stagger to my birthday lunch today, 7 January. Sorry, I meant mine and Amarisse's birthday lunch. Because of course we share the same birth date. She is fifteen today. But I can't believe it – she looks more like twenty-five. While I look about 187…

We had a full turnout, the whole family – me, Amarisse, Sienna, Flora, Richard, Jake, Rosa and Amelia, plus Caitlin and Nigel, who came up specially for the day. And Miranda. A first for her. Shows she is becoming part of the family. She has now met them all. Lucky her.

It is always a rite of passage when a new girlfriend/boyfriend gets to meet her/his partner's family. It's a sign of seriousness and, one hopes, acceptance. I remember going to your house for the first time and meeting your parents. I was scared of meeting your father, Arthur. You had somehow painted him as an ogre. I stupidly tried to ingratiate myself by talking about football, following the flawed logic that because he was a factory worker, he would be keen on football. No such luck. He just grunted and then left the room, leaving your mother, Lily, to give me a cup of coffee and a Carr's Sports biscuit. Remember them? Yummy.

Later, I gathered he had asked you if I was foreign. He

thought I looked Italian. I suppose that was because of my dark hair and rather swarthy complexion. I like to think I am Celtic-looking, in fact. Not any more, of course. My hair is now grey, what remains of it, and I have more wrinkles than swarths.

The venue for the birthday lunch was an Italian restaurant in Highgate Road. I had booked it in advance and paid a deposit. Beforehand, we had birthday cake and the opening of the presents here at my house, in the traditional Davies family way. Then we all walked out through the back garden into the mews to the restaurant. As soon as we got there, I took the waiter aside and said on no account let anyone else pay the bill, except me.

But before we had all properly finished eating and drinking, behind my back, Flora paid the bill – and shared it with her siblings, Caitlin and Jake. I was furious. They can't afford a meal for eleven people – three courses with wine. Whereas I just love throwing my money around...

Guess where I am about to throw my money next? No, not on the West Indies. I have already paid for that, but God knows when we will get there, if ever, as I feel like shit. Since being discharged from the Isle of Wight hospital and coming home, I have tried to be sensible, eating no fats and drinking no alcohol. But I am so worried that my gallbladder will play up again. And then what will I do? Go to A&E at the Royal Free, I suppose, and spend ten hours queuing up, to be told I am too old to be operated on. If the Isle of Wight hospital was frantic, the Royal Free A&E is always a madhouse.

So what I did yesterday was contact my GP's surgery, telling them about my hospitalisation on the Isle of Wight. I asked if they could refer me to whoever is the gallbladder expert at the Royal Free – to save me going to A&E if I get another attack. I eventually got an email from some Camden agency I had never heard of saying they would be in contact sometime, but if I had not heard after three months, I had to contact them. Bloody hell. Then I read that the waiting list for gallbladder ops is now two years. Two effing years. Oh God, I might not live that long.

So I rang my friend the rheumatology consultant at the Royal Free. You will remember how kind he was when you were so unwell towards the end. He cured my arthritis, though I am still injecting myself every two weeks with the miracle drug he put me on about twenty years ago. He had kindly given me his private mobile in case of emergencies, which I take care not to abuse.

On Sunday evening, when I was beginning to imagine that the stomach pains were happening again, I rang him and left a brief voicemail message. I explained my latest problem and asked if he could recommend a gallbladder expert. GPs tend not to know who the relevant hospital consultants are but surely a fellow consultant must. I made it clear I would go private.

He rang back next day and gave me the name of a consultant, whose name I did not catch, and said he would be in touch with me. His secretary rang the day after and gave me an appointment with someone with an Italian-sounding name. I looked him up online and found he was incredibly well qualified – and also possessed Italian film star looks.

The appointment was at the Wellington, one of London's main private hospitals. You once went there in an emergency, at the suggestion of our rheumatologist chum. You had collapsed one Saturday and I took you to see him at a private hospital in north London where he was working that day. He examined you and said you needed an MRI urgently. He was able to book you one at the Wellington on the spot, so we got in the car and drove down to St John's Wood. From memory, the charge for the MRI was £1,500 – and I had to pay it in advance on my Visa card before they would do it. What a liberty.

A brief initial conversation with the handsome Italian would cost me £350, which seemed reasonable enough. All I wanted was a chat with an expert and to ask him a few questions. Most importantly, what could I do to avoid further gallbladder attacks? I did not want him to give me scans or send me for blood tests – they would be expensive and I had had enough of them. I just wanted a simple chat – and some simple advice.

He listened carefully to my account of my recent travails and asked how I felt now. I said I was worried by the prospect of another attack. I asked him if it was likely to recur – and was I really too old to have an operation? He said no, I should have an operation. And he would do it. I immediately felt so relieved. There was no mention of my age or medical history. I did not feel cynical, thinking that in private medicine they will do anything for money. I believed he was right. It was the only thing to do. Have it taken out.

I thanked him and then asked… er, hate to mention it… but how much might it cost? He said that was not his decision, but off the top of his head, he thought around £7k. It was in fact a smaller amount than I had feared. I have a friend who is having his knee replaced privately – a procedure I had done for free fifteen years ago. And he was going to pay £16k. He thought it was worth it, rather than wait forever on the NHS.

I felt I was going against all my principles, jumping the queue and getting ahead of others. Neither of us has ever paid for private hospital treatment. Just as we never paid for our children's education. I do feel that private schools and private hospitals are unfair. I know there are those who would defend me by saying that, by going privately, I will allow someone on the NHS queue to move up one place. But that argument is specious. By going private, I am taking a top consultant away from his NHS work.

Yes, I know most consultants do private work, balancing it with their NHS work. That is the system, and it is perfectly lawful. Yet I still can't justify it. I know the NHS is in chaos – overcrowded, understaffed and with enormous waiting lists. Almost anyone you talk to who needs treatment, rich or poor, will say if they could afford it, they would pay and not wait. It was the thought of a two-year wait that did it for me. When I had my heart bypass five years ago, it was all done on the NHS – at St Bartholomew's, the top place for such things. I don't remember a wait of more than two or three weeks. Things have clearly got worse today. You are well out of it, pet.

I also know that the treatments and the surgeons will probably be the same, whether I go private or NHS. The only difference is you get a private room. And free coffee. I have read stories that the care you receive in a private hospital can in fact be inferior to what you get on the NHS. Your private operation is carried out by a top consultant, but he or she does not supervise the staff who are left to look after you in the same way as would happen in an NHS hospital. The consultant does the surgery, then buggers off back to their NHS work. Or another private hospital. They do not get involved again. That is when neglect can happen. The basic staff in the private hospitals are often agency workers and are no better paid and no better qualified than NHS staff.

Ah well, I have made my decision. My op has been booked. And it is not going to be at the Wellington but at the Royal Free, where the handsome Italian also works. It will be in the private wing, up on the twelfth floor. As I understand it, the NHS will get a whack out of my £7k, as the Royal Free is a public NHS hospital. So you see, I am helping the NHS after all...

The operation takes place on 27 January.

Wish me luck, as I wave you goodbye... Sorry, yet another bad-taste joke.

LETTER TWENTY-ONE

Family party around 2010: (back row) Jake's wife Rosa; Flora;
Margaret; (front row) Jake and Rosa's daughter Amelia; Caitlin
and her daughter Ruby.

Funeral Fun

Wake up, little Susie, I mean Maggie…

While I am waiting for the operation, I have been having some fun, planning my funeral. You never came to your funeral. I mean that you would not have come anyway. You did not want any fuss, any event, any grave, any memorial service. Just like your dad, really. Every time Arthur was poorly, up until when he died at ninety-six, he would say: 'Straight to the crem.' That was what he wanted. No fuss.

Funerals honour the dead, but they are not for the dead, they are for the living. The living decide how they would like to mark the passing of the deceased, and how they would like to remember them. For a few days after you died, I thought I should obey your wishes and do nothing, but then I realised that our family and friends all expected something to happen. So, I contacted Golders Green Crematorium, where most of our locals end up. I booked a chapel for a service, but I did not want it to be conducted by a minister of religion. I would lead the ceremony myself, along with the undertakers, Leverton & Sons of Kentish Town, founded 1789, who would keep me on the straight and narrow. I hoped Caitlin, our eldest, who has the best voice, would say something, but she was too churned up. So Ruby, then aged sixteen and going through a rather naughty phase at school, offered to speak. She did it beautifully, without notes, telling us her memories of you, how she missed you, how she valued you, the way you were always willing to listen to her, without criticising. Jake spoke, but then he is a barrister and it is his job. And I spoke as well. I think Melvyn also said a few words. I chose the music. You had no interest in music, apart from Christmas carols. So I had the choir of King's College Cambridge singing 'In the Bleak Midwinter'. I also chose a Beatles song – 'And I Love Her'. It had me in tears.

I wanted the congregation to exit the chapel, after your body had been consigned to the flames, to the sound of 'Georgy Girl'. You would have been furious, but hard cheese. You were not there. I had discussed it with the present Mr Leverton, explained the reason, that you had written the novel the film was based on – but come the time for the record to be played, it turned out to be a slow and soppy cover version, not the original one by The Seekers. I wanted us to have a sprightly, jaunty exit, not a dirge. I was furious. I complained later to Mr Leverton, who was mortified. By way of apology, he offered to donate £500 to Marie Curie. Wasn't that kind?

Afterwards, we all went back to our house for tea and buns, sausage rolls and sandwiches, wine and whisky. It turned into a rather jolly party. Carmen Callil was there, your old publisher, and Alison Samuel from Chatto.

I also disobeyed your wishes by having a gravestone put up in Loweswater churchyard, along with half of your ashes. Our Lakeland friends and lots of your Cumbrian fans wanted a memorial service in Loweswater church, but I never got around to it. Golders Green was enough. I know from fan letters that many of your readers make a special pilgrimage to your grave in Loweswater churchyard.

Our neighbour and friend Joan in the village sends me a photo every 8 February on the anniversary of your death. Your gravestone always has snowdrops in front. Every year

I am so touched and, without really thinking, I forward this snap to Caitlin, Jake and Flora. Every year, Caitlin and Flora tell me off. They hate seeing your grave. It is too sad. They feel, as I do, that you are still alive.

On the anniversary of your death each year, we have a family lunch in London, just me and our three children, no partners or grandchildren. We walk over the Heath, if my legs are up to it, to look at our seat. It's still there, the one we put up for our silver wedding anniversary in 1985, still the only memorial seat on the Heath to a living person – me. Yes, still here. Just.

And then we go for a lunch somewhere. Last year we went to the Freemasons Arms on Downshire Hill – what a mistake that was. It was a sunny day, and it was so crowded. Not sure where we will go this February. Probably the pub in South End Green, where Amelia used to waitress when she was a student. That's usually quieter.

Every year, I say: why we don't change our annual memorial meal to 25 May, your birthday, which would be a much nicer time of the year to remember you than February, which is a horrible, gloomy time of the year? But they always say no. They want the memorial meal to take place on the day you died.

We try not to talk about depressing things. Instead, we discuss how you would enjoy seeing your granddaughters today, how surprised and pleased you would be by how they have turned out. We reminisce about your orange coat, which you loved so much, and how you could always be spotted miles away across the Heath.

So what am I going to do about my funeral? This is not a bad-taste joke. It's a good-taste joke. I have organised something that I hope will amuse you and all the family.

Whether I am taken to the crematorium or am buried in a

grave, I leave to others to decide. Whether there is a service in a chapel or some other memorial, I don't care. Joining you in your grave at Loweswater church would be neat – and would save money. You and I were so happy in Loweswater all those years. But I do want my funeral tea to be fun. At your funeral tea, it got quite noisy and jolly, but then it just fizzled out. There was no focal point. People just wandered off. Leaving me alone.

I sat there in the empty, echoing house for a long time, feeling desolate, still hearing their voices, but they had all gone. What am I going to do now? How will I cope, living on my own?

You now know, because I have been telling you, all the things I have done and experienced since then, people I have met, places I have been, these last seven years since you died. You are up to date about what has happened to me. Warts and all.

I am sure Caitlin and Flora will be appalled when they read these letters, especially the bits about my lady friends. I like to think you will be interested and amused. And pleased, knowing I have made new friends and not moped at home. You always did say I would be 'fine' and not end up a lonely old git.

For the end of my funeral tea, I have arranged a surprise appearance, by none other than – myself!

Richard has made a half-hour video of me, talking to the family and friends, which will be shown on a screen at the end of my funeral tea. He has been sworn to secrecy – he can't even tell Flora. I address all the funeral guests, and thank them for coming. I say I hope the traffic was not too bad, and that they did not have trouble getting here. I also say that, as this is a video, Richard can send them copies later, if they have to rush off before the end. I hope you enjoyed the show. You've been such a lovely audience, all my life. I'd love to take you home for tea... tra la.

Oh, hold on, you *are* all at home now, my home, in my house, enjoying a sausage roll, I hope, and some excellent Sauvignon Blanc. Why not finish with a nip of whisky, in the Scottish tradition? If it is wintertime, I hope the log fire will be on and we will be having hot food. If it's summertime, I envisage a garden party. With an outdoor screen for the video.

None of us knows when we will go. Well, apart from those like you with terminal cancer, who are given only a certain number of months left. But for most of us, the end is sudden, as it was with Ian Jack.

I don't think I would like to know. I would be counting down the days and it would ruin what time was left. I know some people like to be able to make plans, write letters, get in their goodbyes. Which of course I have done, by making my funeral video.

In the video, Richard has dropped in photos from my life, our life – such as our wedding photo – and also dropped in various clips from family videos over the years. I have suggested to him that he could go on to do this professionally. Follow the format we have created and charge £1,000 for a half-hour film. There must be so many people getting on in life who would like to do this, but don't quite know how to do it, or what to talk about. I will give him a list of topics and questions to be answered.

For example, in the video, I ask myself – why am I doing it? I explain that I always wanted to know more about my mother and father, their early lives, how they met, how they courted, but I never got around to it. My father died when I was eighteen, and I had never had much connection with him. My mother would have told me but I waited too long, till she was in the early stages of dementia. I did try once and all she would say was: 'Oh, I can't remember how I met your faither. Was I married?'

In the video, I tell the story of you and your parents, Lily and Arthur, when you were a stroppy teenager, how you decided you hated your father, believing he was an oaf, so far beneath your saintly mother.

You asked your mother one day why she had married your father. Lily thought for a long time, her face rather anguished and confused, trying to remember. 'Oh, I think he just wore me down...' What a terrible thing to confess to a young teenage girl... whether it was true or not, and it probably was. She should at least have thought of something happy and romantic. After all, they must have had *some* nice times. 'Oh Arthur, he was the handsomest man in the factory. There were always girls hanging around his work bench. You should have seen him on his motorbike. He was so dashing...' Something like that would have pleased you, I am sure. Made you smile. Given you a nice image of their courtship and marriage.

In my funeral video, I also talk about meeting you, chasing after you, being passionate about you, then unable to believe that I was really going out with you – the cleverest girl in the school, the most admired. You were the best thing that ever happened to me. My life turned around totally when we got married.

I also talk about some of the things that have really pleased me in my life. One of them is the fact that all our three children and four grandchildren are each other's best friends. They talk to each other all the time, visit all the time, celebrate family events together, go on holiday together. I know you will be as pleased as I am to hear this. It does not always happen like that in families. There are often feuds and fallings-out – or family members just can't get along together. Arthur worked with his brother Bob in the same factory for forty years on adjoining benches – and they never spoke a word to one another. Some ancient disagreement over money their grandmother left.

My family – *our* family – all seem to get on. I will die happy and smiling if that continues to be the case. What more can we want in life than to leave a happy family behind? They don't have to be wealthy or successful. They need to be healthy, that always helps. But being happy and content, loving each other – that is the best you can wish for.

You hope, as an oldie, that you will be remembered in your family as long as your children and grandchildren are alive. And they *do* talk about you, often – even the young ones. You are not forgotten. You crop up in conversations, especially at birthdays and Christmas. You are an eternal part of our family story.

Just as I will be, when I follow you. But once our children and grandchildren have gone, that will be different. The grandchildren will doubtless hand on family memories to their own children and grandchildren, to the next generation. But it won't be the same. They won't know what you were like. You will just be a name.

It's the same in all families. You live on in people's memories for two generations, then that's it. There's nobody left alive to remember you. It's how it should be, I suppose. How can anyone be expected to be remembered forever? You would have too many people to remember.

But, unlike most of the people on the planet, you and I have left written evidence we were here. Our books might be out of print, out of date, forgotten and unread – at least, mine will be – but they will exist, somewhere. Even if it's only on the dusty shelves of second-hand bookshops and charity shops.

I believe that printed words will last longer than words on the internet. Modern technology dates so quickly. Devices are replaced by new ones and become obsolete. Think of all those trillions of emails whizzing around the world every day. I wonder if, in twenty years' time, anyone will still be able to access them. In my study I have a drawer full of Amstrad discs containing probably a million words, and I now have no idea how to access them. But printed words will live on, somewhere. As they always have in the past. In places like the British Library.

Anyway, see you soon. Can't be long now till I am with you again. Oldies who are widowed always say that, they are looking forward to joining their soulmate. But it is true. In old age, you begin to believe… want to believe… that you will be united again in death as you were in life. We can then have a good chat about the old days. The family. The tortoise.

Or just sit together in silence on your cloud and hold hands. Ah, bless…

Writing these letters to you makes me feel closer to you, until the time eventually comes… In the meantime, I am about to have my operation. Maybe that's the reason for all these maudlin thoughts.

Watch this space. Or just talk among yourselves.

LETTER TWENTY-TWO

Margaret and me in our garden at Loweswater,
around 2000; Mellbreak Fell behind.

Op-ortunity

Here we go again, more hospital stories. Feel free to skip…

Miranda walked with me over to the Royal Free. It's not far – little more than a mile – and I have a season ticket for the place. I always feel much the better for a little walk – on the Heath or along Ryde Sands.

I had been told to report to the hospital at seven in the morning. I thought that paying to go private meant you could have a lie-in, but instead I had to get up at six… ugh.

We went up to the twelfth floor, the private floor, where I had my first Covid test, ages ago now. They had opened it up as they were short of space at the time. At the reception desk, they checked I had paid my £7k up front. I wondered if I would get it back, or a rebate, if I did not survive the op. I was weighed again. Oh God, I am so fed up with being weighed. They have been doing it for weeks, since all this began. I have lost one and a half stones since December. I lost my appetite in the Isle of Wight hospital, which is not like me, as I have been a greedy guts all my life. I have never been fat or even what you might call overweight, I've always been considered a thin person, but over the last year my weight had crept slowly up. Back in December, before I fell ill, I had shot up to almost twelve stone. I blame Miranda. Since we met, we have been drinking loads and stuffing our faces every time we have been together. I have little willpower.

I used to moan about my ever-so-little belly when you were

alive. Funny how you tend to get fat in one particular place. Give up the drink, you always said when I moaned about it. When you died, I started drinking double the amount of wine at supper on my own, sometimes a whole bottle, as I was drinking for you as well. And guess what – my weight went down. Yes, it did, for three or four years after you died. Perhaps with cooking for myself and not eating as much. But then it started to shoot up again.

I was eventually taken to my room, number 13, which was enormous, about the size of a ward at the Isle of Wight hospital. It had a desk, a bed, plus a second fold-down bed and a large window with a nice view. To my annoyance, I failed to identify the view, a rear view of Hampstead houses and streets. I have lived in this area for sixty years, but I just could not work out which streets I was looking at. Somewhere off Haverstock Hill.

Miranda waited with me for a long time, admiring my room and the menu, which was brought in with a flourish by a very efficient-looking young man. There were almost a hundred items on it, including eight different types of soup. I won't eat anything, I said, but she insisted on ticking several dishes which she fancied.

Two hours later, nothing had happened. Nobody had been to see me. I had exhausted my curiosity about the view and was moaning about private medicine and what a swizz it was. But then the anaesthetist slid into the room, rather thin and languid. He stood against a wall, looking even thinner. He asked me the same old questions about my medical history and whether I had any allergies, which must have been recorded dozens of times in the last few weeks. I made my usual pathetic joke about allergies. 'Only Arsenal fans.' He did not change his expression or move his body.

I tried to get him to tell me what time roughly I would be

operated on. Where was I in the queue? He eventually let out that I was going to be the last of the day, which would be at about three or four o'clock. Oh God, and they had made me come in at seven in the morning, just to hang about. Did this mean they were saving a dodgy operation to the last, or an easy one, so they could all slope off to the pub? Don't they realise I am a jolly busy person? I have work to do. Columns to write. A house to run. A lady friend to amuse.

So I sent Miranda away. I told her to walk slowly across the Heath, enjoy the scenery, then do some gentle housework at home and perhaps put the washing on. Before going to bed, she could ring the hospital and find out if I was alive and had had my op. I was sure reception would give her a number to ring. Bye, thanks for coming.

I then fell asleep for about two hours. I woke up to find a porter in my room with a trolley ready to wheel me away – to Nirvana or the operating theatre. I was given the anaesthetic by my thin friend, oh bliss. I do love anaesthetics. After morphine, it is the best thing about all hospitals.

I woke up – goodness knows how long afterwards... several hours later – feeling dopey. When I managed to focus, I sensed a strange atmosphere in the operating theatre. I could hear whispers, mutterings, voices slightly raised, accusations. I thought at first it was my dopey state, still in a dream. Then I picked up that a message had just come up from the laboratories. It turned out that tests showed I had Covid. They had operated on a patient with Covid. Oh. My. God. No wonder there was such consternation.

I had had a Covid test at the hospital two days earlier, swabs and stuff, and again that morning on arrival. But I was supposed to have tested myself in the morning when I left home, which I had not done. Too early in the day. And anyway, I could not face it. I did not want to find out I had

Covid, as my operation would then have been put back for months and I would have had to cancel our Bequia holiday yet again.

So it was partly my fault, for not testing myself; but also the hospital's fault, as the results of their own tests had clearly been delayed.

Too late now. My gallbladder was out. Thank God.

When the recriminations and discussions had died down, and I was cleaned up, I was wheeled back to my Room 13 – still pretty dopey, but pain-free, thanks to all the drugs. Outside my room, a scary notice had appeared, hanging on my door. RESPIRATORY ISOLATION, it yelled, warning anyone not to enter my room on pain of death – well, on pain of becoming contaminated. Anyone who came in had to wear a mask at all times and disinfect their hands when entering or leaving.

Once the anaesthetic wore off, I was in agony, unable to get comfortable, or turn or move. As for the thought of supper, the one Miranda had ordered… it did turn up, but I couldn't face any of it.

In the morning, I woke up to find that Miranda was in my room. She had been able to let herself in. The restrictions on visiting hours you get in NHS wards didn't apply here. So it *had* been worth my going private after all, despite having to get up at the crack of dawn to get to the Royal Free…

Later in the morning, Jake came across and picked me up and drove us home. I went straight to bed and Miranda stayed with me, as I was not supposed to come home to an empty house.

I could not sleep, ached all over, and then I had constipation. For over a week, I mainly stayed in bed, felt awful, and could not sleep. Then I started doing gentle walks on the Heath.

Two weeks after the op, I had to go to the Royal Free again, to see Professor Fusai for a final check-up. I walked there, which was good, my longest walk since the operation. He took off the large plasters covering the three horrible holes they had made in my abdomen in order to extract the gallbladder. It was not cancerous, he said, but it was in a horrible state, infected with something or other. I asked if I could have the gallbladder, in a bottle perhaps. Many years ago, when I had a cartilage out, I persuaded them to give it to me in a little bottle of formaldehyde. I still have it in my room somewhere. But Professor Fusai said they did not do that anymore. Health and safety, probably.

I asked if that was it. Would I henceforth be free of the agony of gallbladder stones forever and ever? He assured me I would have no more gallbladder problems since I did not have a gallbladder anymore. I could drink and eat whatever I liked. The only thing I had to avoid now was any lifting. I said no problem there, squire. I have a fit and energetic young lady friend who does all my heavy and light lifting for me. Among other services. He gave a slightly knowing smile. Well, he is Italian. They understand such things.

So, that's it, pet. The op was a total success. I am ready to go. Bequia, here I come…

And I promise you there will be no more hospital stories or health stuff in any of my letters to you from now on. Scout's honour. DYB DYB, DOB DOB. Or was that the Cubs?

From your awfully old but very fit husband. Oh yes. I still consider myself that.

LETTER TWENTY-THREE

Margaret's grave in Loweswater churchyard. Every year, in February, it is adorned by snowdrops.

Bequia Forever

Sun cream on, pet...

I recovered from my gallbladder operation after four weeks. By being sensible and not overdoing it. Not like me, I know. The Spurs manager, Antonio Conte, had the same op at the same time but he foolishly came back to work after two weeks – and had a relapse.

I had been told to go nowhere for about four to six weeks, which I stuck to. I managed to rebook our Virgin flights for six weeks ahead and change the hotel bookings. My travel agent charged me £400 for each of us to change our flights from mid-January to 1 March, which I considered a liberty. I would have thought that as I was therefore going at a less popular time, the seats would be cheaper. I will never use that agency again. That will teach them. I fussed endlessly about whether to get insurance for the trip as I have always done in the past. But when I admitted I had just had an op and also revealed my long and exciting medical history – and, even worse, my age – the best quote I could get was... £4,000! For just three weeks. Bleedin' cheek. The penalties of age, eh? Miranda, being a young lass of only seventy-six, got her cover for £300. So, we set off worrying about whether something might go wrong with either of us on a small, remote island, with no proper hospital and hellish to get to and get off. And me with no health insurance.

Do you remember Bequia? Of course you do. Titchy island, just five miles long, population 5,000, part of the Grenadines. Near Mustique but nowhere like it. Bequia is a real working island with real people doing real jobs, unlike Mustique, which is now so manicured. I like to think Bequia is like the West Indies in the old days.

You and I always agreed it was our favourite Caribbean island of them all. And together we must have visited around thirty of them over the years since you organised that amazing trip in 1986 on Concorde to Barbados for my fiftieth birthday. I've been back to the Windies every year since. It was twenty-five years ago that we first visited Bequia, never having heard of it before. We were staying at Young Island in St Vincent when we saw an advertisement for a day trip to Bequia on a catamaran.

We were dropped off at a lovely-looking harbour and left to wander around the island for about six hours. We ended up at the Old Fort in the interior, a hotel created by a German couple, Otmar and his wife, Sonia, who had arrived by boat from Europe... and then just stayed. It is a pretend fort, more like a Tuscan stone villa, and ever so romantic with beautiful bedrooms and great food. Sonia was the cook, while Otmar was front of house. We went back there every year for about ten years, for a few days each time, before deciding that Lower Bay, on the harbour side of the island, was the fun place to stay, with six restaurants and cafés within walking distance, and easy access to Port Elizabeth, the island's only town, along the beach and boardwalk. Over the years, we stayed at various places in and around Lower Bay.

We were thrilled when Bequia got a real luxury, top-class, five-star hotel, the Bequia Beach Hotel on Friendship Bay. The Swedish owner, Bengt Mortstedt, still says it was partly because of me. I wrote a travel piece saying Bequia was my fave Caribbean island, but that it was a shame it had not got a boutique hotel. So he built one.

Didn't we have some good hols at the Bequia Beach Hotel, you and me? We would go in January, usually spending just a few days there before moving across the island to Lower Bay.

I continued to go on my own when you were ill. You insisted that your cancer should not ruin my life. And I carried on after you died. I mostly went to Keegan's, which you would never stay at, being a snob. Oh yes, you could be. You thought it looked a bit basic and noisy, which it can be.

Keegan's Beachside Hotel, Apartments and Restaurant was originally a shop, which, over the years, added on rooms and apartments at the back. The name comes from the fact that the husband had been in the merchant navy for many years, working on a British cargo ship, and always remembered the crew raving about someone called Keegan. The footballer. Come on, do concentrate. He thought the name would attract the Brits. It is now run by their son, Messenja. I did once know where his name came from but have forgotten. It can be a bit rowdy on music nights or hog-roast evenings on the beach, which they do each full moon, but I love staying there.

I hoped Miranda would like it. Despite her rather posh background, she is certainly not a snob. More of a hippie really... well, an arty type. She once lived in a shepherd's hut in Cornwall for a whole year.

I was looking forward with only slight trepidation to getting to know her better during the next three weeks. After all, it was only six months since we had first met and we had not properly lived together yet, apart from when I was ill. Would we get on? Would she find out all my faults and irritating habits? I am bound to have some.

We went Virgin upper class, as I am a toff these days. Miranda raved about the Virgin upper-class lounge at

Heathrow, getting out her sketch book to draw the ceilings. After our Concorde trip, you announced you were never going anywhere on long haul in economy ever again. Club class, or you were staying at home. I have stuck to that rule ever since, despite moaning each year about the expense. I like to think it is my only mad luxury in life.

Miranda also raved about the Bequia Beach Hotel, where we stayed for the first few days, again getting out her sketch book to capture the view of the beach from our room. I discovered she always takes it with her, using it as a diary, adding notes and dates. I wish I could draw. One of my regrets in life, along with not being able to play an instrument. You were quite good as a girl at drawing and painting. I once bought you oils and canvas so you could take it up again, but you never did. Miranda not only went to art school, she can also sing and play the guitar. Goodness, what talents.

I remember, when you first came into my life in our teenage years, coming home and telling my mother and sisters how amazing you were: she's so clever, a legend at the High School, bound to get into Oxford, and so talented – do you know she can also paint and draw and is the school's star actress? Oh, and she does public speaking as well, and swims for the school! They always rolled their eyes. 'Is there nothing that Margaret Forster can't do?'

Miranda is turning out a bit like that, with so many hidden talents.

We had supper that first evening in the Bequia Beach Hotel with Bengt and his new partner, Anne. His wife died about seven years ago now, just after you. Each year after that, when we met up, he would give me the latest on his love life while I told him about mine. I do the same with Otmar at the Old Fort. Well, we are chaps of a certain age who have known each other for a long time, even though we only meet once a year.

A few years ago I did a couple of Beatles talks for Bengt at the hotel, proceeds to charity. They still have the posters up at reception. You, of course, refused to attend or ever come to any hotel manager's cocktail parties. You preferred to stay in your room and read. You had heard me talking more than enough times. But it meant you missed the evening that Bengt dressed up in Sergeant Pepper uniform. What a hoot.

Miranda was equally thrilled by Keegan's, which is about a quarter of the price, and with fewer luxuries than the Bequia Beach Hotel, but is ever so genuine, my dear, full of local West Indian families every weekend.

I had expected Bequia to be quieter in March than in January, when I usually go, but we kept bumping into people I knew who have houses on the island and stay there for months every winter. These are the so-called 'snowbirds' from Europe and Canada, who flee to Bequia to escape the cold weather at home. We also met lots of interesting new people. In fact, there were so many social events during our three weeks – such as jazz nights and quizzes at De Reef, the next restaurant along the beach from Keegan's – that Miranda said after the first week she could hardly keep up with all the new people and places. I can, of course, being an exhausting person anyway. I took her to visit Otmar at the Old Fort. I had been emailing him for several weeks, telling him I was coming with a new lady friend, but had heard nothing.

Then I met his son Quirin, who is always known as KingKing, whom everyone on the island knows, and he arranged for us to visit Otmar. He said his dad was looking forward to seeing me again. And Miranda.

Poor old Otmar. Just before Christmas – aged eighty – he had been mugged in Kingstown, the main town in St Vincent. He was checking into an apartment when some youth who had clearly been following him pushed him into the room, beat him up and stole his mobile, wallet and also Christmas presents for his family, which he had just bought. Luckily, Otmar said, the youth did not have a gun or a knife. It could have been much worse.

But he was badly injured and in shock for a while. When we saw him, four months after the mugging, his facial wounds had healed. He was in good spirits, but he did appear to have aged. He was clearly having to make an effort and began to get tired.

He was still living in the same sweet little wooden cottage where you and I visited him many years ago, on the Old Fort estate. The hotel is now an international boutique hotel, available to rent for weddings, parties and conferences. Otmar's cottage is totally isolated, and has wonderful views down the hill to the sea. It is still filled with objects and memories and paintings from his past. All very arty. Miranda loved it and took plenty of photos on her mobile.

Otmar is still living there alone, but Sonia – his blonde German ex-wife and mother of his three children – was at the Old Fort that day. They are long divorced, but she visits each year. Otmar went on to live with Sarah, a local woman, who had been the cook at the Old Fort, and they had two children together. They have now separated, however. The last time I was on the island, Otmar was doing online dating. He's probably not up to that now, after being attacked. And anyway, having turned eighty, he's a bit old for all that nonsense... and I should hope so.

But, of course, you are never too old for that nonsense. As long as you can manage to put one foot in front of the other. Today, I read that Rupert Murdoch, aged ninety-two, has just got engaged to a young woman of sixty-six. It will be his fifth marriage. Good on you, cobber. Oh, hold on, I gather he broke off the engagement after two weeks.

Miranda and Otmar bonded over their experiences of sailing across the Atlantic. Otmar and Sonia had been crew members on a larger boat, whereas Miranda and her husband had sailed their own little home-made trimaran, just the two of them.

Throughout our holiday in Bequia, as we sat with our rum punches at the bar in Keegan's, looking out at the thousand or so yachts that are always bobbing around Admiralty Bay, Miranda explained to me the finer points of yachting, pointing out the different designs, shapes, sails and anchors. She stressed how important it was to be able to recognise navigation lights in the dark. I could barely see them, let alone understand what they meant. Miranda has much better eyesight than me.

Every day she tried to spot a trimaran, without success. But then we found out that there was an old trimaran – the *Gusto* – doing charter trips to places like Tobago Keys. We booked it for a day trip to Mustique. I had not been there for years, though you and I did stay there a couple of times, in the Cotton House.

Miranda, being a fit, strong young woman of seventy-six – or have I said that already? – kindly gave the three-man crew a hand with putting up the sails and pulling in the sheets. I concentrated my efforts on the rum punches. Jolly hard when you are in full sail and both the boat and your stomach are heaving.

The *Gusto* is fifty feet long, and was carrying ten passengers that day. It is bigger than Miranda's *Sweet Painted Lady* trimaran, which was only thirty-nine feet long and pretty cramped, by the sound of it. In the 1970s, they had none of the modern devices and navigation aids all yachts have these days. All sails and anchors had to be raised by hand. They did not even have a radio.

She loved being on a trimaran again; it brought back memories. It was probably her biggest treat of the whole holiday – well, apart from eating out every night at excellent beach restaurants, meeting all my friends and exploring the island. We walked along the coast all the way to Port Elizabeth on three separate occasions, taking a whole morning each time. It is quite a hilly route, and there are some steep wooden steps on the boardwalk, but – with lots of stops and drinks at the rum shacks on Princess Margaret Bay – I managed it. I had feared my days of doing that walk, which I have always loved, were over. But will it be the last year I can manage it? I hope not.

So how did we get on, I hear you asking.

One of the things we did on our walks, and out drinking, was people watching. Imagining the passing lives. Miranda is excellent on accents, particularly rural Norfolk and northern. We got into the habit of making up the conversations the couples going past were having. Miranda always began it, with a funny, stream-of-consciousness monologue, and I tried to keep up. Such as? It would be pointless to try to recreate them out of context. They would not be funny. But at the time we were both in hysterics at our own wit, like two silly schoolgirls (or should that be silly schoolboys?). One evening, we stayed at home in our cottage at Keegan's and Miranda cooked a sumptuous meal of fresh tuna, bought that morning at the harbour in Port Elizabeth. We had it on our balcony, looking out at the sea and the stars. And the navigation lights. She laid out a tablecloth, using one of her scarves, and produced a written menu.

We pretended she had just opened a new beach restaurant and I just happened to be her first customer, who had newly arrived on the island. We kept up the role-playing for an hour, to our own amusement. Miranda had worked as a waitress in Chelsea many years ago, when she was a student, so she played the role to perfection. I had a stab at talking like Giles Coren, the *Times* restaurant reviewer, who is a friend of mine. As was his dad.

What I did not know, before this holiday, was just how witty and funny Miranda can be. In company up till now, meeting my family and friends, she had let me make all my usual jokes, show off and tell stories. But with just the two of us, and no audience except me, she turned out to be exceptionally creative and imaginative. Also – wait for it – she can do bird noises. Beat that.

Remember all those years ago, back in 1960, when our landlord, Mr Elton, took us to a Crazy Gang show and one of the items on the bill was a woman doing bird noises? We had hysterics. It was so stupid and silly.

Something else I did not know about Miranda, till the hols, is that she loves dancing. In fact, we danced together at most meals, if there was music.

You and I never danced together. It was one of the first things you said to me, when I met you at a sixth-form youth club in Carlisle. 'Can I have this dance?' I asked. 'I hate dancing,' was your reply. 'That was not my question,' I said.

At family parties, over the years, I used to dance with Caitlin and Flora, and then our granddaughters, until they got too old and embarrassed. I know I am rubbish at dancing. I'm still doing my sixties grandad jive, which becomes stiffer and more wooden with age. Miranda is more modern and floaty, lithe and rhythmic. But I do enjoy dancing. And now I know she does too.

All in all, Miranda and I got on wonderfully well. We bonded in many ways and had some good laughs. There were no cross words between us. We enjoy the same things – walks and talks, outings and events, food and drink (she has a very good appetite). She's also an all-round enthusiast: she loves the bare wooden benches at Keegan's as much as she does the posh décor at the Bequia Beach Hotel, enjoys the roadside jerk chicken in town just as much as lobster at an expensive restaurant. One of the things I love about her is that she never moans or criticises.

And nothing went wrong: no accidents or illnesses. Well, apart from in the last couple of days when the sea turned a lot rougher and we were both bashed and bruised by stupidly trying to swim against big waves. I used to love big waves, throwing myself into them with the children in Portugal. Now I am so stiff and slow I fear something will break if a big wave hits me.

Oh, there was one incident I promised Miranda I would not mention to anyone. One evening, Miranda had too many rum punches and was a teensy bit unwell. She blamed the rum punch, but I suspect it was something she had eaten. Anyway, I mopped it all up. Only fair, really, as she looked after me so well after my operation. And in Bequia, helping me onto boats and planes, carrying my bags, even my mobile phone. I would never have been able to go on my own, or have managed without her.

But, as I said, nothing at all serious happened, to either of us. Being sick was trivial. So I saved £4k on the travel insurance I never took out...

So will it last? Are we together for what is left of my life?

Miranda's Memoir, 'My Name Is Not Matilda', did get finished, without any more tears, and I hope you will enjoy it. Amazon does deliver to heaven?

Holidays in exotic, tropical places with sand and sea and constant skies of blue, and in lovely company. Is it all too good to last? I'm keeping my fingers crossed that it will. I am indeed a very happy, lucky boy. And I hope you will be happy for me as well, that I am happy.

I don't deserve it, of course, a second go at life, having had such a wonderful, fulfilling, productive, exciting, stimulating, loving married life with you for fifty-five years.

I never thought I would be so happy again, after you died, or have such a compatible lover and soulmate. Or of course still be alive at eighty-seven.

Looking around at our friends in the neighbourhood, the ones we both knew so well for so many decades, it seems to have been the blokes who have died first, leaving their wives alone. I am unusual and not typical.

So, up in Heaven, when you next see God... sherry evening, perhaps, or afternoon tea at His place... tell him how well I am doing, and pass on some of my chat, however trivial, however personal. But perhaps change some of the names. I suspect some of the saints and angels sitting at His right hand, or hanging around the Pearly Gates, might well be wee clypes, as my mother used to say. But I am sure God himself keeps secrets.

Do thank Him on my behalf. I will never take for granted my good fortune, which alas you never properly had. You had a great life, yes, and a lovely, loving family, and I like to think an adoring, grateful, kind husband. You were creative and successful, admired and loved, happy and content, but in the end your last years were rather grim. Unlike me, you were deprived of the fun and entertainment of reaching your eighties, the joys of seeing your grandchildren grow up, having all the pleasures and stimulation of an active – if sometimes rather staggering – old age.

See you again soon...

Tarra for now. Love always – Hunter.